SEXUAL HARASSMENT IN OUR SCHOOLS

What Parents and Teachers Need to Know to Spot It and Stop It!

ATLANTIC COMM. COLLEGE

—◦—

Robert J. Shoop
Jack W. Hayhow, Jr.

Allyn and Bacon
Boston • London • Toronto • Sydney • Tokyo • Singapore

ISBN 0-205-15319-4

This publication is designed to provide accurate and authoritative information in regard to the subject matter covered. It is sold with the understanding that neither the author nor the publisher is engaged in rendering legal, accounting, or other professional service. If legal advice or other expert assistance is required, the services of a competent professional person should be sought.

From a Declaration of Principles jointly adopted by a Committee of the American Bar Association and a Committee of Publishers.

Printed in the United States of America

10 9 8 7 6 5 4 3 2   97 96 95 94

We dedicate this book to our children,

Allison B. Shoop and Brian J. Hayhow

Contents

How Would Your Child React?
How Would You React?

Situation: Heather and Jennifer are walking down the hallway during passing period between classes. Four boys walk up to them and begin making lewd comments. As the boys pass the girls, one of the boys reaches over and grabs Heather's breasts and squeezes them.

Situation: As Latoya walks down the hall two boys stop on either side of her and sandwich her between them. They keep her between them for about 15 seconds, rubbing her up and down.

Situation: Jim, a middle aged male high school teacher, is standing in the hallway as the students pass between classes. As Stacy, a shy sophomore, walks toward him, he yells out, "God, I can't wait till summer to see you in a bikini."

Situation: Mr. Smith is a favorite teacher among the male students. He has a "sexy" joke or story to tell every day. Today he passes out a cartoon from a pornographic magazine.

Situation: Mr. Green has a habit of putting his hands on the female students. He grabs them on the upper arm or shoulder and sometimes puts his arm around them. He tells several female students that he really enjoys it when they wear short skirts to class.

Situation: Megan is in kindergarten. She is the last student to get off the school bus at the end of the day. Every day as she walks past Mr. Smith, the bus driver, he either gives her a hug, pats her on the bottom or gives her a piece of candy.

Situation: Several eighth grade boys shout obscenities while two of their friends pull down Nikki's slacks as she walks down the middle school hallway.

All of these situations are examples of real life events that are occurring in our schools every day, and each of these situations is an example of sexual harassment. This book will show you how to help your child recognize and deal with sexual harassment. It will also show you how to work to make sure that this type of behavior does not take place in your child's school.

Preface

We wrote this book because sexual harassment is rampant in our schools. While this revelation is in itself disconcerting, the long-term consequences of this aberrant and hostile behavior are even more shocking. We'll briefly describe these appalling consequences in Chapter One and explore them in depth in later chapters. This book will point out and support one unassailable fact: *The costs and consequences of sexual harassment in our schools are extreme.* They are extreme in the devastation of our daughters. They are extreme in the dysfunctional and counter productive manner in which our sons are socialized to relate to their mothers, sisters, wives, female friends, and coworkers. They are extreme to our economy, to our ability to compete in the world marketplace, and even to the American standard of living. For these reasons eradicating sexual harassment in our schools is an urgent priority.

As we began to consider how to eradicate sexual harassment in our schools, we couldn't help noticing the prevailing attitudes and ideas about the subject. Generally speaking, most people are not certain exactly what it is. Even though newspapers, magazines, radio, and television are overflowing with coverage of sexual harassment, the average person is hard pressed to describe specific behavior that constitutes sexual harassment. Fewer still have an understanding of the causes and consequences of sexual harassment, or the methods of preventing it. What little understanding and knowledge does exist is likely to be based upon incomplete and often sensationalized reports about sexual harassment litigation. While an understanding of the legal aspects of sexual harassment is important, we believe this is only part of the larger picture. Law, and the punitive consequences of breaking the law, speak to preventing and punishing the overt behavior of sexual harassment. Laws and punishment do little, if anything, to help us understand the underlying causes of the behavior. To an overwhelming degree, the law treats the symptoms and ignores the disease. That model seldom works in the medical community and it is similarly ineffective when applied to sexual harassment.

In addition to understanding the legal aspects of sexual harassment, we need to understand the personal and interpersonal causes and consequences of sexual harassment . We need to see sexual harassment for what it really is: *A flashpoint in the continuum of contentious relations between men and women, boys and girls.* It is critical to understand that sexual harassment does not occur in a vacuum. It occurs as an instinctive and predictable result of people in conflict. Until we resolve this underlying conflict between women and men, the specter of sexual harassment will be ever present.

The purpose of this book is to help resolve the conflict between the sexes. Our effort is organized around three cornerstone ideas: (1) The new conception of sexual harassment as a flashpoint in the continuum of contentious relations between men and women, boys and girls. (2) Awareness of certain specific circumstances that have conspired to fuel the flashpoint. (3) With effort, education and training, people of all ages can learn a better way to live.

We have focused on eliminating sexual harassment in our schools for several very important reasons. The most obvious and compelling reason is that the school-age victims of harassment are the most vulnerable. Perhaps there can be disagreement surrounding the behavior of adults, but there can be no question that our children should be safe and unafraid. It is our responsibility as parents, educators, or citizens to protect our children while we teach them how to protect themselves.

This book focuses on schools for another reason: We don't believe people suddenly begin harassing as adults. This destructive behavior is learned, and it is learned to a dramatic extent, in our schools. Because it is more difficult to change the attitudes and behaviors of adults, we can't effectively combat the true causes of sexual harassment if we wait until adulthood. To eradicate sexual harassment we must begin by teaching people a better way to live very early in life. We must use our educational system. Our schools can and must do more than teach math and science. They must help our children become happy, productive, and cooperative members of society. For us to do less is to shirk our responsibility and invite disaster. We'll talk about solutions in our schools because that's where many of the answers are.

We hope that you will give some of your time and attention to this critical issue. Only by doing so can you come to understand the pervasive nature of sexual harassment in our schools and the devastation that ensues.

Acknowledgments

This book is the result of several years of study in the area of sexual harassment in elementary and secondary schools. Although we alone are responsible for the content of this book, we have profited immensely from the research of others and from discussions with friends, colleagues, public school teachers and administrators, and elementary and secondary school students.

We would like to thank several people for their special help. We especially want to thank our friend, colleague, and collaborator, Debbie Edwards for her counsel and advice, especially in developing the material in Chapter Seven. We thank Bill Pryor for his friendship and for being a significant component of our thought process. We'd also like to thank Cheryl Brown Henderson. Her early and constant support, as well as her commitment to the cause of gender equity, has been inspirational, instructional, and much appreciated. We thank Jayne Richmond and Linda Thurston for their early support and encouragement for this project.

We would also like to thank Kathy Navarre and Mark Neish, who provided research assistance. Special thanks go to Katha Hurt, Joyce Hayhow, Mary Shoop and James Shoop for reading and commenting on the entire manuscript.

Jack would especially like to thank Dr. Esther Markus. Over quite a number of years and in many different circumstances, Esther has helped me to think about people and their relationship with one another. Her insight and guidance have been extraordinary.

We also thank Ray Short, senior editor at Allyn & Bacon, and Steve Dragin, Associate Publisher at Allyn & Bacon, for their commitment to this book.

Cover photograph is a digitized enhancement from the video program *Sexual Harassment: What Is It and Why Should I Care?*, cinematographer Bill Pryor, and is copyrighted by Quality Work Environments, Inc. Cover model is Katherine Pryor.

Introduction

It's another typical day at the middle school. Several male students prowl the halls like lions ready to pounce on their prey. Other young men brazenly stare at the bodies of each of the female students as they pass in the hallway. The girls try to ignore the comments about their anatomy. Their venture to the girls' restroom becomes a groping session. Males squeeze the females' bottoms as they try to pass by. In the boys' restroom a boy reads graffiti on the wall about one of his female classmate's supposedly insatiable appetite for oral sex.

Sexual harassment, a long overlooked but serious problem in our schools, is not about flirting, or humor, or raging hormones, or horseplay. It is about power and the offender's need to exert power over a victim.

Sexual harassment has probably always existed. However, until recently this offensive behavior had no name; and without a name, it was difficult for victims to confront their harassers. Females often thought the offensive behavior was something that was happening to them individually. Sexual harassment was seen as a personal problem rather than a social issue. Without a name sexual harassment was treated as an unavoidable fact of life in a world dominated by males.

In the 1960s and 1970s women began talking among themselves about the shared experience of unwanted sexual overtures. As women talked about their various experiences, they began to notice a common pattern. Many had quit or been fired from jobs because they had been made too uncomfortable by the behavior of men. In 1974 Lin Farley coined the term sexual harassment to describe the pattern of unwanted sexual attention by males to females in the workplace.

Farley identified sexual harassment as a violation of the concept of equality, and the neutrality of the workplace. She was the first to address the psychological, sociological, ideological, ethical, legal, and economic consequences of sexual harassment. Like many injustices which had an impact primarily on women, many people initially thought sexual harassment was of negligible concern.

Until very recently, women who were sexually harassed at work were told to put up with it or quit. Over the past ten years society has gradually come to recognize that women and men should not have to endure sexual harassment in the workplace or in schools. During the early 1990s the televised Supreme Court confirmation proceedings of Clarence Thomas, the national debates generated by the Navy Tailhook scandal, and the well-publicized charges of sexual harassment by elected officials brought the issue of sexual harassment to the attention of the general public.

Sexual Harassment In Our Schools

Although sexual harassment in the workplace is recognized as a serious issue that must be addressed, there is another environment in which even more insidious and outrageous sexual harassment occurs. The nature and extent of sexual harassment in elementary and secondary schools is only beginning to become known. Sexual harassment in schools is different from sexual harassment in the workplace because: (1) students are required by law to remain in school and (2) because of their age, students are more vulnerable than adults. Not only are administrators and teachers sexually harassing each other, but they are also sexually harassing students. It is perhaps more surprising and distressing that students are sexually harassing their classmates, and even their teachers.

In 1993, the first scientific survey of student sexual harassment was commissioned by the American Association of University Women Educational Foundation. The results of this survey document that sexual harassment has reached epidemic proportions in America's schools. According to Anne Bryant, executive director of the AAUW Educational Foundation, "Sexual harassment takes a toll on all students, but the impact on girls is devastating." For example, according to a "fact sheet" issued by the AAUW, the consequences of sexual harassment for girls include:

> *(1) School girls are more frequently and more likely to be sexually harassed in school than boys, (2) Girls are more likely to be harassed in public places, (3) Harassment has an exceedingly negative effect on girls' academic participation and performance, (4) Sexual harassment has a significant impact on girls' emotions and their feelings about themselves, and (5) Girls who have been harassed at school tend to try to avoid it happening again, even if it means restricting their choices of where to go or who to be with.*

Sexual Harassment is Under-Reported

Despite the growing awareness of the problem of sexual harassment, most victims still do not report it. According to the above mentioned survey, students usually do not report sexual harassment to adults. If they tell anyone, most tell a friend. Only seven percent of sexually harassed students told a teacher, and almost one quarter of the victims told no one about being sexually harassed. Many victims do not report it because they are afraid that they will not be believed. Some are concerned that their friends will ridicule or ostracize them. And others simply do not want to draw attention to themselves. Many victims of sexual harassment do not understand that they have the right to be free from intimidation and hostility.

Many victims would rather try to deal with sexual harassment informally first but do not have the skills. In the workplace, victims of sexual harassment are just as likely to change jobs as a result of sexual harassment as they are to take formal action. Students usually do not have the option of leaving school, so they suffer in silence also.

Today there is a national discussion taking place to determine appropriate and inappropriate behavior in schools. Clearly the rules for appropriate behavior in schools are changing. It is no longer acceptable to excuse inappropriate behavior as the natural activity of adolescent boys. It is equally clear that there is a great deal of confusion and controversy regarding exactly what the new expectations are. Sexual harassment is a complex and perilous issue. Charges of sexual harassment deal with very sensitive and personal issues and are often hard to prove. Students, parents, teachers, and administrators are asking their friends, colleagues, and family members: "What exactly is sexual harassment?" "How pervasive is the problem?" "Who are the victims of sexual harassment?" "Who are the harassers?" "What should I do if I am sexually harassed?" "How do I keep from being falsely accused of sexual harassment?"

There is a tendency to think of sexual harassment as a women's issue because nine out of ten formal complaints of sexual harassment are filed by women. In the majority of these cases the harasser is a man. However, the AAUW survey of sexual harassment in our schools indicates that significant numbers of boys report being targets of sexual harassment in school. However, because the vast majority of reported cases of sexual harassment involve male harassers and female victims, and because the impact of sexual harassment is greater for girls than boys, we will focus much of our attention on sexual harassment that involves male perpetrators and female victims. Although we often use the male pronoun for the harasser and the female pronoun for the victim, it must be remembered that both sexes can be harassers and victims.

Most men don't think of themselves as sexual harassers. However, surveys indicate that the majority of men say they had done or said something that a woman might interpret as sexual harassment, even if it was unintentional. Often, when men are questioned about sexual harassment, they react with fear, anger, confusion, exasperation, indignation, or resentment. This is not difficult to understand when one remembers that, with much justification, men are characterized as the oppressors and women as the oppressed.

It is not our intention to place blame for sexual harassment. We believe that most men and women oppose discrimination and believe in fairness. We also believe that most men and women will join in efforts to eradicate sexual harassment from our schools because it is the right thing to do.

The vast majority of teachers and administrators would never willingly harm the students with whom they work. Many teachers and administrators are actively working to make all schools places where boys and girls have an equal chance to learn and to grow into happy and productive citizens. However, sexual harassment is an issue that was not discussed when most teachers and administrators were trained. Until very recently, it was not mentioned in professional literature. Educators, parents, and others must work together to increase their understanding of the extent and seriousness of sexual harassment in our schools. They must come to understand the devastating impact of sexual harassment and work to remove it from our schools.

It is critically important that every school district have a formal plan for eradicating sexual harassment. This plan must include a written policy prohibiting all forms of sexual harassment. The policy must clearly identify unacceptable behavior and be widely distributed throughout the school district. All school employees and students must know that sexual harassment is prohibited and that there will be serious consequences if harassment occurs. School districts must also have educational programs on sexual harassment for their students, parents, faculty, and staff. We must prepare our daughters and sons to know their rights and empower them to stand up for these rights. We must educate our sons and daughters to respect themselves and their fellow students.

Goals of This Book

This book is written for parents, students, educators, and anyone else who is concerned about healthy environments within our schools. The four goals of the book are (1) to help parents and students understand the nature of sexual harassment, (2) to help parents and students understand the causes of sexual harassment, (3) to help parents and students understand the consequences of sexual harassment, and (4) to help parents, students, school board members, and state legislators eradicate sexual harassment in our schools.

Our schools can only improve if people care. Sexual harassment will disappear from our schools only if students, parents and educators choose to remove it. Before we can eradicate sexual harassment we must understand the forces that have created it. To do this, it will be necessary to understand gender discrimination, so that each student and parent can help their schools foster, nourish, and achieve gender equity for all students.

The book will be successful if there is an increase in the number of schools that value the worth of each individual and agree that all people are equally human. In order for this to occur each of us must accept the responsibility to: (1) learn about sexual harassment, (2) find out if sexual harassment is occurring in our child's school, (3) teach our male and female children to understand that sexual harassment is wrong and must not be tolerated, (4) teach our children what to do if they are sexually harassed, and (5) make sure that our children's schools have a comprehensive program for eliminating sexual harassment.

Part One
A Better Way To Live

I am only one; but still I am one.
I cannot do everything, but still I can do something;
I will not refuse to do the something I can do.

Helen Keller

Chapter One

A New Understanding

In recent months only the most confirmed recluse could remain unaware of sexual harassment. From confirmation hearings for the U.S. Supreme Court to the halls of Congress, from corporate board rooms to our most cherished religious organizations, from our armed services to ivy covered campuses, and even in our grade school and high school classrooms, sexual harassment has been intimated, alleged, denied, litigated, and too often proven.

At times it seems that the news media scrutinizes our every utterance for signs of sexual harassment. A recent sample from a mid-size metropolitan daily newspaper revealed almost 100 articles about, or references to, sexual harassment during a 60-day period. Magazines, radio, and television are equally consumed by the topic. With the possible exception of AIDS, it is difficult to recall a social issue that has captivated our national attention to this extent.

Why is there so much interest in sexual harassment? Certainly, it is a serious concern. It causes grave damage to the emotional and physical health of its victims. It damages reputations and it destroys careers. It deprives people of the rights granted by the U.S. Constitution. Without question, it reduces our national productivity and undermines our standard of living. Yet, in all candor, there are other threats that are equally destructive but receive comparatively little attention. What is it about sexual harassment that so captures our interest?

It would be logical to think that citizens are concerned because of the obvious detrimental effects sexual harassment has on people and their lives. We believe, however, that society's concern about sexual harassment is more related to the human condition in America in the 1990s. Essentially, we believe the issue of sexual harassment crystallizes society's fear and frustration regarding relationships with members of the other sex.

To have this idea make sense, it is necessary to expand our understanding of sexual harassment. In order to promote this understanding, we will first explore the currently accepted definition of sexual harassment. We will discuss behavior that can be construed as sexual harassment from a legal standpoint. Then, we will step back from legal considerations and think about sexual harassment from a personal and interpersonal perspective. It is from this perspective that we begin to understand sexual harassment as *a flashpoint in the continuum of contentious relations between men and women, boys and girls.*

The Legal Parameters of Sexual Harassment

In the most practical of terms, sexual harassment is any unwelcome behavior of a sexual nature that interferes with your life. There are two primary components to this definition. The first component has to do with the idea that in order to be considered sexual harassment, behavior must be "unwelcome." The term "unwelcome" indicates the action or behavior was unsolicited and nonreciprocal. In other words, the person witnessing or affected by the behavior didn't "ask for" or invite the behavior, nor did the person respond "in kind" with similar behavior. For example, wanted kissing, touching, or flirting, is not sexual harassment.

The second component of the definition is the term, "behavior of a sexual nature." This term includes virtually any conduct that refers to sex. Such conduct can include using profane language or telling off-color jokes. It includes using sexist terms such as "babe" or "sweetheart," or making comments about body parts. But, it can also include what some may consider to be "terms of endearment" such as "honey," "baby," "darling," etc. Behavior of a sexual nature includes leering and ogling, and without question, any kind of unwanted touching such as patting, hugging, and pinching. Finally, any request for sexual favors in return for benefits meets this criteria.

Courts have held that sexual harassment is discriminatory behavior that violates Title VII of the Equal Rights Act of 1964, Title IX of the Education Amendments of 1972, the Fourteenth Amendment to the U. S. Constitution, and various state and local human rights acts. Title VII prohibits discrimination in employment. Even though Congress passed the act in 1964, it was not until 1979 that Catharine MacKinnon, a law professor and a pioneer in the development of sexual harassment legal theory, conceived of sexual harassment as a form of sexual discrimination. Although the concept of sexual harassment is not completely settled in law or fully understood by society as a whole, courts have clearly and consistently affirmed that the workplace and the school must be free from sexual harassment.

Title IX was enacted to combat the widespread discrimination against women in all aspects of education. It protects students in educational settings from sexual harassment in essentially the same manner that Title VII protects employees in the workplace. In the 1992 landmark case of *Franklin v. Gwinnett Public School District*, the Supreme Court ruled that schools can be held liable for monetary and compensatory damages resulting from a teacher's sexual harassment of a student. While the facts of the case spoke exclusively to teacher to student harassment, the *Gwinnett* decision has generally been interpreted to hold that schools are liable for all types of harassment, including student-to-student, teacher-to-teacher, and student-to-teacher. The 14th Amendment of the U.S. Constitution provides for equal protection for all people. This amendment essentially says that a person's rights cannot be taken without due process of law.

While not legally required to do so, the courts tend to look to the Equal Employment Opportunity Commission (EEOC) for guidance on matters relating to sexual harassment. In 1988 the EEOC issued a document to all field offices entitled *Policy Guidance on Current Issues of Sexual Harassment.*. The document outlined the behavior that constitutes sexual harassment. The guidelines reminded field personnel that sexual harassment is a form or subset of sexual discrimination and is therefore prohibited by Title VII of the 1964 Civil Rights Act. The guidelines went on to say that:

> *Unwelcome sexual advances, requests for sexual favors and other verbal or physical contact of a sexual nature constitute sexual harassment when (1) submission to such conduct is made either explicitly or implicitly a term or condition of an individual's employment, (2) submission or rejection of such conduct by an individual is used as the basis for employment decisions affecting such individual, or (3) such conduct has the purpose or*

effect of unreasonably interfering with an individual's work performance or creating an intimidating, hostile, or offensive working environment.

Three distinct forms of sexual harassment have evolved from the EEOC guidelines and from recent court decisions. Often these forms overlap or occur simultaneously. However, each is a distinct category and provides for a separate complaint or cause of action. The following is a brief introduction to each category of sexual harassment.

* ***Quid Pro Quo*** - *Quid pro quo* is a Latin term often used in law. It means, essentially, "you do something for me and I'll do something for you." In the context of sexual harassment of students, *quid pro quo* may mean sex for grades or other favors. *Quid pro quo* includes an offer of special treatment such as awarding a better grade in return for sexual favors. It can also be a threat of retaliation. For example, *quid pro quo* occurs if a teacher threatens to lower a grade or refuses to write a letter of recommendation because a student rejects a sexual request. *Quid pro quo* also takes place if a teacher threatens a student with some penalty if she does not consent to have a sexual relationship with him. One critical aspect of *quid pro quo* is that a single event constitutes a violation. If a teacher makes a sexual proposition that involves the student's educational conditions even one time, *quid pro quo* sexual harassment has occurred. In *quid pro quo* sexual harassment the deprivation of educational benefits, once such deprivation is proven, allows the victim to ask the court to provide relief.

It should be noted that the discussion of *quid pro quo* in schools broaches the subject of teachers having sex with students. This is, of course, a critically serious concern. It raises questions regarding rape, sexual abuse, sex with a minor, and other equally serious issues. These topics involve areas of law other than sexual harassment and will not be discussed in this book. While most discussions about sexual harassment remind us that in order to be considered sexual harassment the sexual attention must be unwanted, in the school context there is another consideration that is more important. Because most students are minors, the issue of welcomeness is not the appropriate consideration. Teachers and students should be prevented from any sexual contact on the basis of the professional obligation that teachers have to act in the place of the parent while the child is in the care of the school. In addition to interfering with the teaching process and violating the trust that is necessary in a teacher-student relationship, it is ethically abhorrent.

*   **Hostile Educational Environment** - Hostile educational environment is the most prevalent and misunderstood form of sexual harassment. For practical purposes, any sexually-oriented conduct or any sexually-oriented atmosphere that is intimidating or offensive to a reasonable woman, can be construed as creating a hostile educational environment. The concept of hostile educational environment is so confusing because men and women often perceive the very same behavior in quite different ways. What a man might consider innocuous, a woman might consider blatantly offensive. It is important to remember that courts now tend to favor the victim's point of view.

The opinion of a "reasonably prudent woman" is considered in the court's decisions. One critical dimension of the hostile educational environment category is that sexual harassment can occur even though the victim does not suffer any loss of economic or tangible benefits. Unlike *quid pro quo*, hostile educational environment requires a consistent pattern of behavior. A single event does not necessarily constitute a violation. In order for sexually unwelcome and offensive behavior to be considered to have created a hostile educational environment, the behavior must be "sufficiently pervasive and severe." The EEOC drew upon a substantial body of judicial reasoning in holding that Title VII affords the right to work in an environment free from discriminatory intimidation, ridicule, and insult. The student's workplace is school, and consequently students are afforded this same right.

   * **Sexual Favoritism** - Although many authors categorize sexual harassment as either *quid pro quo* or hostile environment, we believe it is helpful to identify a third category, sexual favoritism. Although sexual favoritism is a manifestation of a hostile environment, it has some important distinctions and can therefore be viewed as a separate category. Sexual favoritism occurs when a student receives preferential opportunities or benefits as a result of submission to a teacher's sexual advances. In these circumstances, a student who is having a consensual relationship with a teacher, or who is voluntarily engaging in flirting behavior, may be given special treatment in the form of higher grades or other benefits. Given this situation, it is the other students (who are not receiving the same preferential treatment as the student involved in the relationship) who are the victims of sexual harassment.

Reasonable Man Versus Reasonable Woman

   In later chapters we will spend more time discussing the standard that courts use to determine if sexual harassment has occurred. However, at this point a few words need to be said about the difference between the reasonable man, and the reasonable woman test. In cases of negligence the courts have historically asked "what would a reasonable man (sometimes modified to 'reasonable person') do in a similar situation." For example, if a person walking down the sidewalk in front of your home was injured as a result of falling into an unmarked hole that was created by your effort to repair the sidewalk, a court would likely rule that you are liable for the injury to the walker. This decision is based on the belief that a "reasonable person" in a similar situation would have been able to foresee the likelihood that the hole presented a danger. This reasonable person would then have taken steps to warn pedestrians of the hole and thus prevent the injury.

In early sexual harassment cases many courts examined behaviors offensive to women in light of this test. As we mentioned earlier and will discuss later, men and women often see the same situation quite differently. Therefore, because many men did not see anything wrong with the allegedly offensive behavior, courts often ruled that the behavior did not violate the "reasonable man" standard, and therefore no harassment took place.

Recently courts have begun to hold that the appropriate standard in sexual harassment is, "would a reasonable person of the same sex as the victim, in most cases a woman, find the behavior unreasonable?" When we present training sessions on this aspect of sexual harassment, men often say, "If I didn't mean anything offensive, how can it be sexual harassment?" Men also express resentment and confusion because they say, "How are we to know what to do? One woman may thank me for a compliment, and another may get angry and charge me with sexual harassment." One way to gain some understanding about this dilemma is to look at the concept of comfort zone.

Comfort Zones

Although courts are beginning to define sexual harassment from the perspective of the person who is being harassed, a few things must be said about how women perceive sexual harassment. Not all women perceive all of the same behaviors as sexual harassment. A study conducted by Beth Schneider revealed that over 92% of the women surveyed viewed sexual assault, sexual propositions, and pinching or grabbing as sexual harassment. However, only 64% viewed being stared at or looked over as sexual harassment, and only 53% saw joking about a person's body or appearance as sexual harassment. This study indicates that there is some ambivalence and little consensus among women on what constitutes sexual harassment in their day-to-day interactions. Slightly less than 50% viewed touching or hugging as sexual harassment and only one in four women considered requests for dates to be sexual harassment.

All people have a series of comfort zones that they draw around themselves. Normally, in our interactions we allow people to get closer and have more personal interactions only as we feel more comfortable with them. In a casual conversation with a stranger we are likely to share little personal information, allow no touching, and keep a fair amount of space between ourselves and the stranger. As we feel more comfortable with a person and get to know them better, we are likely to allow them to stand closer to us, perhaps put a hand on our shoulder and even joke or tease us. It is only our dearest friends or family members that are given permission to enter the closest circle of intimacy.

We accept the behaviors of others and reciprocate those behaviors only if they fall within the comfort zone that we have developed with that individual. Each of us have different comfort zones. We each select who will enter our comfort zone and for what purpose. Problems can arise when we think that because we have included someone in our comfort zone, they have an obligation to include us in theirs. For example, a female student may indicate that she is upset because a male acquaintance, seeing her in distress, put his arms around her and gave her a hug. Clearly, in this situation the boy meant no harm; in fact, he was offering kindness. However, the girl responded by pulling away, or might even accuse the boy of sexual harassment. Another male student may make the same gesture and the same girl will appreciate his thoughtfulness and return the hug. She has a friendship that allows her to feel safe with the second boy and is therefore willing to allow him into her comfort zone.

In another situation, a close male friend might tell a female student, "You look really nice in that sweater," and she might feel complimented. She has allowed him inside of her comfort zone by giving him permission to comment on her physical appearance. However, another male student may make a similar comment and the same girl may put it outside the comfort zone and be offended.

Sexual Harassment as a Flashpoint

In science, a flashpoint is defined as the lowest temperature at which vapors above a volatile combustible substance will ignite. In human relations, a flashpoint is the point at which someone erupts suddenly into action. Both concepts are relevant to our discussion. It doesn't take a great deal of imagination to view male-female relationships as volatile and combustible. And we have all, no doubt, observed circumstances where someone suddenly erupts into action. The fact that both men and women are often perplexed by such eruptions further frustrates our attempt to define what legitimately constitutes sexual harassment.

In order to understand sexual harassment as a flashpoint in the continuum of contentious relations between men and women, boys and girls, we must abandon the idea that sexual harassment is an isolated event which occurs in a vacuum. Instead we must see sexual harassment as the point at which a volatile combustible substance (the fears and frustrations inherent in male-female relationships) will ignite and cause someone to erupt suddenly into action.

Let's explore the idea of a flashpoint in the continuum of contentious relations between men and women, boys and girls.   A continuum suggests an on-going progression of elements that vary individually by small, perhaps minute degrees. That seems to be an appropriate characterization of the nature and structure of many relationships.

Now we move to the core element of our new concept about sexual harassment, contentious relations. The dictionary definition of *contentious* as exhibiting an often perverse and wearisome tendency to quarrels and disputes. We can think of no more telling description of what we observe, study, and unfortunately, often participate in ourselves. A review of best-selling book titles, talk show topics, and daily conversations reinforces the premise that much of the interpersonal exchange between women and men is contentious in nature. That men and women exhibit often perverse and wearisome tendencies to quarrel and dispute is undeniable.

We view sexual harassment as far more than an isolated rude affront or a single hostile attack. Instead, we see it as the most obvious manifestation of relationships fraught with misunderstanding, uncertainty, frustration, and fear. To a very large degree, sexual harassment is the predictable result of women and men in conflict. As we've said before, until the conflict between men and women is resolved, sexual harassment will be a tragic part of life.

It seems to us, if we want to understand the conflicts in our relationships, it's important to first understand ourselves. It's helpful to take an objective look at why we do what we do. Much has been written about the psychology of human motivation. While we don't intend to review that vast body of literature, we would like to make this observation: *people seem to want their own way, and, they usually want it right now!* That may seem overly simplistic, but don't you find it to be true? If you think back to some of the problems you've experienced with other people, you'll probably discover that in almost every circumstance, what you wanted was in conflict with what the other person wanted. That's why you had a problem! If what the other person wanted didn't interfere with what you wanted, there would have been no problem.

Men and women often want different things. That's how we enter into the continuum of contentious relations. We'll talk later about the specific differences between what men and women want, but for now let's operate under the premise that in many cases, the differences are extreme.

Perhaps the first conflict between a particular woman and a particular man is not of major consequence to either person. There is probably a small wedge driven into the relationship and some residual negative perception for each, but in the greater scheme of things, no great harm is done. The value systems of both people remain intact, and each will continue to attempt to achieve his or her own goals. When the next problem arises, there is not only the problem at hand, but some history of contention as well. Perhaps at this point someone gives in, or perhaps someone has the power to achieve dominance. Maybe the disagreement escalates. Whatever the resolution, or lack thereof, the personal relationship between the individuals deteriorates because the people involved are so focused on the conflict they can see little else.

As you can imagine, the next contact between these two individuals is likely to be tense and stressful. Lacking common ground or any significant understanding of each other's feelings, both tend to protect vigorously their own position and psyche. Winning (whatever that may mean) becomes paramount. Negative feelings and attitudes may lead to progressively hostile personal interactions. Rudeness, overt hostility, verbal, and physical abuse can then seep into the relationship.

In moments of conflict combatants may tend to indict each other on the basis of their sex. If this happens, full scale sexual discrimination develops. According to Gordon W. Allport, "Few people keep their antipathies entirely to themselves." Prejudice will somehow, somewhere find expression in action. These actions have distinguishable degrees that range from passivity to extreme violence. We have used Allport's stages of prejudice as a way of describing how milder forms of sexual harassment, if left uncorrected, may develop into more serious forms.

Contentious relations, including sexual harassment, occur along a continuum. They follow a pattern similar to Allport's five stages of prejudice. Allport's stages of prejudice and our parallel stages of sexual harassment are as follows:

(1) Antilocution - talking negatively about a group. We doubt that much can be done to intervene in the private conversations of men about women. However, it is in these conversations that the

seeds of sexual harassment are planted. Locker room humor, sexist jokes, and ribald stories lay the foundation for men to consciously and subconsciously think of women only in sexual terms, and more specifically, in terms of derision and ridicule.

(2) Avoidance - making conscious efforts to avoid members of the disliked group. Historically we have taught boys that there are boy activities and girl activities. Many boys are still conditioned to stay away from activities that are stereotyped as feminine (i.e. dance, music, art, poetry, etc.) Because they are discouraged from such interaction with females, boys have little first hand experience with girls as equals.

(3) Discrimination - undertaking to exclude all members of the group in question from certain types of employment or other social privileges. Courts have made significant progress in eliminating "male only" social and professional groups. This is very helpful, because by keeping women out, these groups reinforced the separateness between men and women. It is easier to discriminate against an outsider group than it is an insider group.

(4) Physical attack - personal attack and other forms of violence or semiviolence. Sexual harassment is a form of attack. Whether it is verbal or physical, it harms people. It is our belief that most boys and men would not sexually harass women if they had a better understanding of how their behavior hurts women. Physical assault and rape are the most extreme form of physical attack.

(5) Extermination - the ultimate expression of prejudice. We are not comfortable making the leap to this last stage of prejudice. However, it is obvious that some sexual violence ends in the murder of the victim.

Although Allport did not claim that his five-point scale is mathematically constructed, he used it to call attention to the enormous range of activities that may result from prejudice. Although many people will never move from antilocution to avoidance, or from avoidance to a higher level on the scale, *activity on one level makes the transition to a more intense level easier.*

Sexual harassment often emanates from these contentious relations. In this context, sexual harassment may be used as a way for men to express hostility or anger. Men may also harass to demonstrate their power or to compensate for their lack of power. This form of harassment can be particularly destructive because it is often directed at a victim who was not involved in the original conflict. The victim of the harassment is, many times, a woman in a subordinate position to the harasser and, generally a person with limited resources to defend herself. So we see that conflicts between men and women have the potential to provoke widespread harassment.

We also find that what we call cultural conflict causes trouble in relationships between men and women. These cultural conflicts relate more to the structure of our society than to any personal enmity. Underlying these cultural conflicts are preconceptions about "the way things should be." For example, some men still cling to the belief that women should be "barefoot and pregnant." If a man holding such a belief finds himself in competition with a woman for a promotion, he may respond with inordinate hostility. Even though the hostility is caused by the societal structure that allows women to compete with men, the competing woman, or other women, will bear the brunt of the hostility. Often this hostility takes the form of sexual harassment.

In Chapter Two we will explore volatile combustible substances, those problematic elements of relationship and circumstance that conspire to create the flashpoint of sexual harassment.

Chapter Two

Causes of Sexual Harassment

In the past, people probably didn't think much about sexual harassment. For one thing, the term did not exist. Of course, there was some hanky panky in the office and certainly the ever present "dirty old man" lurked about. In schools there were rude boys and teachers with "Roman hands," but even in the most obvious circumstances, these objectionable actions were generally viewed as personal problems rather than employment or educational problems. A women or a girl often thought the offensive behavior she experienced was happening only to her, and because the offensive behavior had no name, it was difficult for her to confront her harasser. Sexual harassment was generally treated as an unavoidable fact of life in the workplace and in the school yard. Until very recently, when students complained about the harassing actions of their fellow students, they were told to ignore the behavior or to avoid the offending students.

Today the prevailing attitude is radically different. Over the past ten years society has gradually come to recognize that women should not have to endure hostile conditions in the workplace or at school. Behavior that was formerly attributed almost exclusively to individual misconduct has been classified (correctly) as a societal problem. The problem is so rampant that at times it approaches the level of sexual warfare. For example, the 1993 AAUW report on sexual harassment in our schools reports that sexual harassment is an experience common to the vast majority high school students. "Clearly the most alarming finding of the survey is that fully four out of five students report that they have been the target of some form of sexual harassment during their school lives." Of those students who reported experiencing harassment, "one in four report being targeted 'often.' " According to this survey, "A student's first experience with sexual harassment is most likely to occur in the middle school/junior high years....(however,) some students first experienced unwanted advances before the third grade." How in the world did this happen? And why?

The obvious questions emerge. Has sexual harassment always occurred? Have men always abused women in the workplace? Have boys always abused girls in school? Was sexual harassment prevalent even before we knew what to call it? We'll be the first to admit that we're not absolutely certain about the answers to these questions, and we're aware of no valid research that can provide the answers. However, we do have a sense that in recent years the problem has increased significantly. We believe there are some very simple and obvious reasons for this increase. There are also some hidden agendas, some not so simple and obvious reasons that fuel the flashpoint of sexual harassment.

What Causes Sexual Harassment?

There are a lot more women in the workforce today than ever before. At a very basic level, more women in the workplace translates directly into more interaction between men and women. More interaction between women and men logically leads to more opportunity for conflict. As simple as it sounds, that's one of the most significant factors involved in the burgeoning phenomenon of sexual harassment.

There is, of course, more to it than that. As women have entered the workplace in increasing numbers, many have earned positions of authority and prominence. That they have done so in the face of substantial obstacles not encountered by their male counterparts is often remarkable. However, it is this success and achievement that many times fuels the flashpoint of sexual harassment. The success of women in the workplace and the power over men inherent in this success has in many cases created confusion, frustration, uncertainty, and fear among men. Seldom are these uncomfortable feelings directly articulated or even acknowledged. Instead they are acted out, often by means of sexual harassment or other hostile behavior. Many times this hostile behavior is directed not at the woman in a position of authority but at other, less powerful women in and out of the organization.

The Power Paradigm

We believe that sexual harassment is more about power than it is about sex. To a very large extent, people adopt the attitudes accepted by and expressed within their culture. Children raised in German speaking homes naturally speak German. Children raised in abusive families are more likely to abuse their own children. Boys and girls raised in an atmosphere of male dominance and female subservience tend to accept those roles as right. Children who are raised in homes where women are treated as "second class citizens" take these attitudes and behaviors to school with them.

The outmoded idea that females are naturally dependent on males may have come from the image of the savage cave man dragging a cave woman by the hair. Whether or not this image has any basis in historical fact, it is the image that best symbolizes the view of the aggressive man and passive woman. According to Marilyn French and others, the earliest people probably lived in small cooperative communities where the sexes shared roles and had equal status and respect. Perhaps because of their greater upper-body strength, men gradually took over the role of hunter. This gave men a role in society that developed into exclusive hunting cults. This male solidarity excluded women from hunting. Patriarchy, the institutionalization of male supremacy, gradually developed and spread.

While the species and the civilization have evolved considerably in a few thousand years, powerful vestiges of male dominance are alive and well. Even though few women need protection from rampaging beasts, the deeply ingrained idea of man as the powerful protector of woman has been a compelling and pervasive component of every little boy's education and socialization. Our society aggressively insists that men should have power and authority over women. We absolutely instill in our male children the idea that power over women is a basic right and responsibility of manhood.

One of the most blatant examples of the perpetuation of male dominance and female subservience is seen in Helen Andelin's book

Fascinating Womanhood. This book was written for the instruction of young women. As you read the following quotes keep in mind that they are from a 1992 edition of the book.

> *"Feminine dependency is the feminine actions of a woman. It can best be described by saying, 'It is her lack of masculine ability.' The role of man, we have learned, is to lead, protect and provide for woman. Her need for his manly care is called feminine dependency.*
> *Don't think that protecting a dependent woman is an imposition on a man.* **This most pleasant sensation a real man can experience is his consciousness of this power to give his manly care and protection. Rob him of this sensation of superior strength and ability and you rob him of his manliness.***(original emphasis) It is a delight to him to protect and shelter a dependent woman. The bigger, manlier and more sensible a man is, the more he seems to be attracted by this quality."*

The back cover of this book announces that, *"Fascinating Womanhood* offers guidance for a new generation of women, happy, fulfilled, adored, and cherished, who what to rediscover the magic of their own feminine selves." With "more than two million copies in print," we can't help but wonder how many hundreds of thousands of boys and girls are being influenced by these ideas. The above paragraphs are representative of the message presented in this book. In addition to telling young women that men want to protect dependent women, Andelin tells women how men feel in the presence of capable women.

> *"What happens when the average red-blooded man comes in contact with an obviously able, intellectual and competent woman manifestly independent of any help a mere man can give and capable of meeting him or defeating him upon his own ground? He simply doesn't feel like a man any longer. In the presence of such strength and ability in a mere woman, he feels like a*

futile, ineffectual imitation of a man. It is the most uncomfortable and humiliating sensation a man can experience; so that the woman who arouses it becomes repugnant to him."

We could take some comfort if we could discard the above comments as isolated remarks by someone from an ancient civilization. However our society, whether we intend or not, still teaches our sons that lack of power over women makes them less of a man. We teach our children that boys get to make the rules and girls must obey them. The many methods, subtle and blatant, conscious and unconscious, by which this occurs are discussed later in this book. However, a recent conversation we had with a colleague serves to illustrate the point:

"My daughter has always been a leader. She has been a member of the student council and was the president of the council at her middle school. At first she was pleased when she was elected to the student council in high school. However, after attending several parties where some of the boys laughed at her and told her 'girls may think they can rule the world, but they can't,' she decided that she was not interested in continuing in student council next year."

Given these deeply ingrained correlations between male dominance and masculinity, is it any wonder that a 50-year-old male teacher reporting to a female principal for the first time in his life feels uncomfortable, or that male students resent and resist being led by females? Adult males in the workplace and young males on the playground face a painful paradox. Their very definition of manhood involves power over women, and yet they find themselves answering to female bosses or being told that a girl is going to be the captain of their team.

A Reasonable Explanation for A Most Unreasonable Behavior

Given these deeply held beliefs about male dominance and masculinity, we can understand how uncertainty, confusion, frustration, and fear are often translated into hostile action. Given the volatility of the situation, what response can we predict?

The answer is pretty simple and straightforward. Virtually every discipline of the human sciences has at one time or another addressed the instinct toward fight or flight. In this regard, "human nature" displays a remarkable consistency. When a man, whose self concept revolves around power over women, is faced with a drastically different reality, he feels threatened. He may see his choices limited either to battling the perceived threat with whatever weapons he has available or retreating from the threatening environment.

Men make both choices every day. The workplace and the school have changed, and many men and boys don't like the changes. The new configuration of authority between men and women has resulted in many men lamenting that "things just aren't the way they used to be." Many men take early retirement (voluntary or involuntary) because they rebel against the new order. Many valuable and well-trained employees resign and move on, hoping it will be different somewhere else. In our schools, boys pressure girls to stay out of certain classes and activities. When girls do gain admission to formerly all male activities, boys sometimes drop out. In the workplace the direct and indirect dollar costs of these flight responses are enormous. In our schools the costs are immense.

Running from the threatening environment may require substantial effort and time, but the fight response can be initiated at once. Often this fight response takes the form of sexual harassment or other forms of sexual violence.

While we are in no way condoning this behavior, we can, with objective evaluation, begin to understand how and why this hostile behavior occurs. As long as the paradigm of male dominance and female subservience is perpetuated, as long as men accept the idea that power over women is integral to the masculine role, and as long as men perceive female authority as a threat, sexual harassment will continue to permeate our society.

Boys and Girls Are Different

While common usage has obscured the difference between the words sex and gender, we use sex to refer to biological and anatomical differences that cannot be changed while we use gender to refer to socialized or cultural differences that can be modified. However, in quoting other authorities, we will use the terms they employ.

All people, regardless of race, creed, ethnicity, physical challenge, mental challenge, or sex, are worthy of equal dignity, opportunity, and respect. Men and women are equal with regard to these fundamental rights, but they are not the same. To operate under the illusion that men and women are the same is foolish and potentially quite damaging. According to Stephen Bergman and Janet Surrey, "while it is crucial to begin discussion about breaking down stereotypes, it is equally crucial to acknowledge differences in experience, perceptions, and power. Denial interferes with dialogue, engagement, and real understanding. It is critical to distinguish stereotype from difference."

Some of our differences are individual, expressed person by person. Other differences appear most strikingly across cultures. And, some of our differences are gender-related. According to psychologist David McClelland, "Sex-role turns out to be one of the most important determinants of behavior; psychologists have found sex differences in their studies from the moment they started doing empirical research." In many cases, gender-related differences are the core ingredient of female-male conflict. For that reason, awareness of these gender-related differences becomes critically important.

Very few adults are immune to the frustrations emanating from gender-related differences. Virtually everyone has, at one time or another, been bewildered by the attitude or behavior of a person of the other sex. We are often astonished that what we see as obvious, seems invisible to the other person. It is this disparity of perception that lurks at the heart of some (and probably most) male-female conflicts. The truth is, men and women experience the world differently. Men and women bring contrasting expectations into every situation and relationship. "How should people act? What is right?" These questions are answered differently by women and men.

These differences of opinion occur because women and men are trying to accomplish widely varied goals. A seemingly simple, straightforward conversation, for example, serves a far different purpose for a typical woman than a typical man. According to sociolinguist Deborah Tannen, many men tend to see the world as a hierarchial social order where they are either "one up or one down." In this world view, our simple, straightforward conversation becomes a competitive negotiation to determine who assumes dominance in the hierarchy. According to Tannen's theory, the objective of conversation for men is to gain the upper hand and resist attempts from others to push them around. For men, life is very much a struggle to preserve independence and avoid failure. On the other hand, according to Tannen, many women see the same conversation as an opportunity to initiate or strengthen a connection. For many women conversation is a way to achieve closeness. Talking provides the opportunity to seek and give confirmation and support. For many women, life is community. The struggle within the sphere of the community is to preserve intimacy and avoid isolation.

Tannen suggests these differences can be understood in a framework of status or connection. Men are continually attempting to achieve and maintain status; women are continually attempting to establish and maintain connection, to include themselves as a part of an interdependent group. Men, in attempting to achieve status, take aggressive action to demonstrate how they are different (better) than others. Women, because of their desire to be a part of the group, minimize differences and promote egalitarian attitudes. To men, independence is foremost; to women, intimacy is foremost.

Given these widely divergent ideas and objectives, it's easy to see how there is often disagreement about what is right and how one should act. A woman, naturally evaluating a man's behavior from her own perspective and motives, may well interpret his pursuit of status as arrogant, sexist, or cold. A man, evaluating a woman's behavior from his own perspective and motives, may well interpret her pursuit of connection as irrelevant, nonproductive, or emotional. That ill will emanates from these conflicting viewpoints is hardly surprising.

It is surprising, though, how early in life these dissonant manners of relating to the world emerge. Casual observation reveals that at a very young age, boys and girls tend to play in different ways. Boys tend to play in large groups, often outside, with one boy leading and the rest following. The hierarchy is established and maintained by the boy who can give the orders and make others follow. Boys play games with rules, games that almost always have winners and losers. And, in an effort to attain status, even in the early years, boys will often boast and argue about their skill.

Girls, on the other hand, play in small groups or in pairs. They often negotiate the rules which are generally subordinated to the feelings of each individual. Most of the games have no winners or losers. Girls often just sit together and talk; they seldom boast or challenge each other directly. The differences in girls' and boys' play was well stated by Jean Piaget when he suggested that boys' games are more concerned with rules while girls' games are more concerned with relationships. The differences most of us have observed in the play activities of boys and girls have also been documented by research conducted by Janet Lever. According to her "these differences are readily apparent and seemingly ingrained by the time children are 10 years old." But the differences may, in fact, emerge much earlier than that. According to the studies of Robert Stoller, gender identity, that unchanging core of personality development, is "with rare exception firmly and irreversibly established for both sexes by the time a child is around three years old."

The question that springs immediately to mind is, how and why do these nearly universal differences between the sexes occur? The answer is so obvious and logical that we may over look it. Almost without exception, women are primarily responsible for early child care. In simple terms, from the first moments of life, girls have the feeling that "I'm like you, we're connected." Carol

Gilligan, in her ground breaking book *In a Different Voice*, suggests that "...girls, in identifying themselves as female, experience themselves as like their mothers, thus fusing the experience of *attachment* with the process of *identity formation* ..." (emphasis ours). The concept of being a woman is inextricably woven into the experience of being connected to other people. What is right and what a person should do rest on a foundation of attachment.

The experience for male children is quite different. From the first moments of a little boy's life, he has the experience of "I'm different from you; we're separate." As a result, according to Nancy Chodorow, male development involves a "more emphatic individualization and a more defensive firming of experienced ego boundaries." The concept of being a man is firmly rooted in achieving and maintaining separation. What is right and what a person should do rests on a foundation of independence.

Again, we can easily recognize how these divergent views about what is right provide the impetus for misunderstanding and controversy. There is, however, another gender-related difference that may contribute even more to cross-gender belligerence. It reveals itself in what Gilligan describes as moral choice. Through the observation of moral choice, we can glimpse the difference in how men and women perceive the world, how they make choices based on those perceptions, and how they behave as a result of the choices.

According to Gilligan, men and women tend to make moral choices, deciding what is right and what they should do, using different criteria. She suggests that women tend to embrace a care perspective while men tend to employ a justice perspective. She believes that female decisions are based primarily on the resulting effect of those decisions on other people. The fundamental questions in a care perspective would appear to be...How does this decision make other people feel?   What impact will this action have on other people? Gilligan concludes that "...women not only define themselves in a context of human relationship, but also judge themselves in terms of their ability to care."

If women are concerned with care and responsibility, men seek answers to what is right and what they should do (moral choices) in a context of rights and rules. If the rules dictate a certain decision, the feelings of the people involved have little relevance. Central to a justice perspective are the questions... "Does this decision conform with the established rules?" And ... "Is this fair?" Clearly, these distinctly different decision making criteria, can and do lead to different conclusions and actions, and may provoke quarrels and hostility.

We also find that men and women often have a much different response to problems or what Judith Jordan refers to as "painful affect." According to Jordan, "Women often want the man's presence and acknowledgement, the witnessing of their feelings, while a man often seems propelled into action to change or remove the 'offending feelings.' Women often attune to and want sensitivity to feeling, while men tend to focus more on action." Men often don't understand why women "want to talk about something until they beat it to death," while women can't comprehend why men don't need to "process" the event or feelings.

We were reminded of this easily observable gender difference while talking to a woman about her relationship with the male executive to whom she reported. The woman is the publisher and chief executive of a weekly business newspaper in a major metropolitan market. When describing how she worked with her immediate supervisor, she laughed out loud and said,

> *"I've finally learned. When I want to talk to this guy about something, I start like this: 'I want to tell you something but I don't want you to do anything. I've already fixed the problem, so you don't have to worry about it or figure out what to do. I just need to talk to you about it.'"*
>
> *She continued with her story, "Before I learned to say that, I was always so frustrated because he immediately jumped right in there to fix the problem. I know he was trying to help, but I didn't want him to fix it, I just wanted him to listen and to understand."*

Once again, we can see how the difference between men and women can set the stage for conflict. We have observed this same behavior in classes that are traditionally male dominated, and which are taught by males. We were observing a furniture construction class that had two female students and fourteen male students. Each time one of the female students asked the teacher for some help, the male teacher would not make suggestions, offer advice, or give encouragement. He would step in front of the student and proceed to fix the problem. We can't be sure if this behavior was based on the teacher's belief that the female students were genetically incompetent and it would thus be a "waste of time" to teach them, or, if the teacher's need to be in control outweighed his responsibility to teach. In the same class we observed that when male students asked for help, the teacher only offered minimal physical assistance. The teacher sent the clear message that the boys could "figure it out" for themselves.

Finally, we have discovered that what men perceive as threatening is quite different from what women perceive as threatening. Referring once again to Gilligan's work, we find that men and women may perceive danger in different social situations. Men are more likely to construe danger in situations of intimacy or personal affiliation while women feel threatened by isolation. It seems reasonable that if men aspire to independence, situations involving affiliation and intimacy would be threatening. One response to such a threat could be aggression which might take the form of rudeness, overt hostility, sexual harassment, or even physical attack. While we certainly cannot predict an exact response when intimacy threatens a man's primary goal of independence, we should not be surprised by retaliatory behavior.

Sex-Role Stereotyping

Social scientists borrowed the term *role* from the French theater, where it referred to the roll of paper that contained the actor's part. Today we see a role as the pattern of behavior that a person is expected, encouraged, or trained to perform. According to Deborah David and Robert Brannon, roles involve very few exact behaviors. They are usually clear but general guidelines regulating how a person should behave. Just as actors consciously learn the role that is written by the playwright, children learn their roles by observing adults. They also learn from others who are playing complementary roles.

David and Brannon believe that learning how to "play the role of male or female" is the most complex, and demanding role that children must learn. Children start learning their roles at birth and spend a good part of their lives perfecting the assigned sex-roles. The costumes, props, and rewards are quite different for boys and girls. From the time a newborn baby girl is wrapped in a pink blanket and her brother in a blue blanket, the two children are treated differently. Baby girls are often treated as if they are much more fragile than baby boys. Many times toddler boys are told, "Big boys don't cry," while toddler girls are cuddled at the first whimper or sign of a tear. While these incidents may not by themselves produce ill effects, they are indicative of a pattern of differing expectations for each sex. We all recognize how quickly children learn what is expected of them.

Where there is some tolerance for "mistakes" in how boys and girls learn their roles as young children, there is much less tolerance during adolescence. As parents of teen-age children, we are acutely aware of how cruel teen-agers can be to their peers who don't dress, walk, speak, look, eat, or relax in the "acceptable" way. Sex-roles and sex-role stereotypes are forged and tempered in the crucible of middle school and high school.

This realization increases in importance when we recognize that to a large extent sex-role stereotyping is so deeply woven into the fabric of our society that most of us are not even aware of it. In fact, most people think of these roles as innate and genetic rather than learned. Sex-role learning is the only explanation for such behaviors as boys holding doors open and girls wearing make-up. This unconscious learning begins to harden into unexamined behaviors and expectations for the behaviors of others. Boys learn that the masculine role includes the fact that they belong to the superior sex. Strong-willed girls challenge sex-role stereotyping at the risk of having their spirits broken. After studying societies all over the world anthropologist Margaret Mead concluded that:

> "Many, if not all, of the personality traits which we have called masculine or feminine are as lightly linked to sex as are the clothing, the manners, and the form of head-dress that a society at a given period assigns to either sex...the evidence is overwhelmingly in the favor of social conditioning."

Children interpret the world and their place in the world from their surroundings. They learn how to conduct themselves by watching the people in their lives. If parents and teachers expect boys to play baseball and girls to play with dolls, that is what the children are likely to do.

Now there is absolutely nothing wrong with boys playing baseball and girls playing with dolls. However, if boys are taught it is unmanly to play with dolls, and girls are taught it is unfeminine to play baseball, the children will begin to define themselves by what they do rather than by who they are. If, when these children go to school, their parents and teachers expect boys, but not girls, to be interested in math, we have a serious and far reaching problem. The critical point is that our common, socially acceptable expectations tend to limit what children can accomplish. Our expectations, what we can very correctly identify as sex-role stereotyping, can and do rob children of opportunity. While this is true for both sexes, it is more true for girls. Society seems to embrace a lot more "girls can't, or shouldn't" ideas than "boys can't or shouldn't " ideas. For example, society often communicates the message that, "girls don't do very well in science." This message is sent so often and in so many ways that fully capable girls tend to stay away from science courses. This denies girls the opportunity to study science, and later denies them as women the opportunity to participate in science-related professions. Most parents and most educators are not consciously trying to deny opportunity to female children. Instead, they are products of the conditioning of their own parents and teachers.

Sexism

The concept of sexism, is fraught with emotion, controversy, and misunderstanding. But to exclude the topic from this discussion would be to ignore a major component of the sexual harassment phenomenon.

> *A father and his son were in a car accident. The father was killed and the son seriously injured. The father was pronounced dead at the scene of the accident and his body taken to a local mortuary. The son was taken by ambulance to a hospital and was immediately wheeled into the operating room. A surgeon was called. Upon seeing the patient, the surgeon exclaimed, "Oh my God, it's my son!"*

Were you perplexed by the story above? Even slightly, even for a moment? Because many of us process information on the basis of sex-roles, we failed to associate the concept of surgeon with the concept of woman. Therefore, some of us were momentarily confused. We wonder how the patient could be the surgeon's son when we know the patient's father is dead.

Sexism is often an unconscious ideology, a set of beliefs that we accept implicitly, without question. We're usually unaware of the acceptance of such beliefs because we can't conceive alternatives. Sexism is a prejudice based on a faulty and inflexible generalization about members of one sex. A sexist person is one who uses sex as a criterion to make evaluations and normative judgements about another person.

> *In the conference room of a major, international engineering firm, several staff members were meeting to discuss problems with a particular contract. In attempting to explain the circumstances of the job, a*

*middle manager remarked to a vice-president, "You
know this is a tough job."
    The vice-president replied, in all earnestness, "If
it were easy, we would have given it to a woman."*

It would be depressing enough if this were an example of the
way it used to be.   Unfortunately, this is a verbatim report of a
meeting held in 1993. Sexism has the effect of placing women in an
inferior position. The prejudice and stereotyping inherent in sexism
(coupled with a culture that embraces the concept of male
dominance) causes many men to view women as less than their male
counterparts. This perception of women as inferior seems to
provide some men with the belief that they have license to abuse and
denigrate women through attitude, language, and physical conduct.
Such treatment can range from excluding women from work groups
to sexual harassment to rape. In Chapter Three we'll explore the
pervasive evidence of sexism in American culture. We'll see how,
from the moment of birth, sexism begins to rob female children of
their health, opportunity, security, and dignity.

For now, it is sufficient to understand how the gross
injustice of sexism can contribute to contentious relations between
men and women. Because the impact of sexual harassment is
greater on women than men, it is difficult for men to comprehend
it's true nature and effect. If you are a man, try to imagine how you
would feel if you were passed over for promotion after promotion
because of your hair color. Think about how you would react if you
were right-handed and throughout your life you were told that only
left-handed people could excel as managers. What if the people who
were holding you back were almost always women? Would that
seem fair? Would you harbor animosity toward the female sex?

Sexism is one of the most significant factors in the
contentious relations between men and women and, consequently, to

the perpetuation of sexual harassment. If we are really interested in protecting our children; if we really believe that all people are worthy of equal opportunity, dignity, and respect; and if we are really interested in a better way to live; then we must come to understand the devastating role sexism plays in our lives.

An Early Lesson In Sexism

Allison's pigtails bounced up and down as she ran to the car, opened the door, hopped up and slid onto the front seat. I enjoyed picking her up from school and taking her to her sitter. Mary and I, like most parents, were anxious for her first year of school to go well. We believed that a good first experience with school would go a long way toward ensuring future successes. We were both nervous about sharing teaching responsibilities with someone we didn't know. We had many questions: Will her teacher be competent? Will she like Allison? Will Allison do well in school? Will she like school?

As she fastened her seat belt, I asked her how her day went.

"Great, I like school! Mrs. Lamb let me help her collect the lunch money today!"

"Do you know any of the other kids in your room?"

"Oh, yes! Kristin's desk is right next to mine, and Andrea and Ben and another kid from T-Ball are in my class, too."

"What else did you like about school today?"

"Well, we played dog again."

"Dog? I don't think I know that game. How do you play it?"

"It's lots of fun. The girls that are playing stand next to one of the boys. Then a boy throws a stick across the playground, and the girls race each other to fetch it. The girl who gets to the stick first brings it back to the boy."

Perhaps I was jumping to conclusions. I took a deep breath and said, "Oh. That's an interesting game. Do the girls ever get to throw the stick?"

"No, just the boys. It's fun. I like to run around."

I caught my breath and could feel myself becoming anxious. We had raised Allison to believe that boys and girls are equal. We had taught her that she can become whatever she wants to be. We tried to use only nonsexist language and to help her understand the consequences of sexism. Equity was not just talk in our house. Allison had helped stuff envelopes for women political candidates and had marched in NOW demonstrations. Now, after one week of kindergarten, she is fetching sticks thrown by boys!

During the rest of my day that conversation kept running through my head. I could not stop thinking about how many lessons that are taught and learned in school are not in the curriculum guides. I became more and more concerned as I thought about how each lesson learned creates the foundation for future lessons.

There is another aspect of sexism and sex-role stereotyping that can be very damaging. It has to do with the messages we communicate in schools about the proper role and importance of women in our society. As one example let's consider the seemingly harmless activity of an all-girl cheerleading squad. First, we need to acknowledge that there are a number of very positive elements involved with cheerleading. However, we also need to be aware of other not so positive messages inherent in this activity. In many ways cheerleading communicates that the proper role for girls is to cheer the boys on to victory. The central concept of female cheerleaders for male sports is that boys are responsible for achievement and girls are responsible for supporting the boys.

We think it's terrific for students to support one another. But, if the issue is support, why don't we have all-boy cheerleading squads leading the cheers for the girls' basketball team? Just as in the story about Allison and the game called Dog, some school activities create the perception that girls should be subordinate to boys. The social structure in many schools strongly suggests that girls should support boys as the boys strive to achieve.

This message can be subtle, or as is true in the following example, this message can be blatant. During a discussion about sexual harassment in schools, a high school teacher related this story.

> *"I teach in a school where the athletic program has a fund raising event every year. The female students are expected to participate in a 'slave day.' During this day, boys bring dog collars and leashes to school and lead the girls around as the girls carry the boys' books and do their other bidding. Many of the girls wear signs that say, 'So-and-so is my master."*

We think this is a pretty strong example of the way schools teach girls that they are somehow less competent than boys, but we wanted to know what girls thought of this practice. We conducted a survey of two hundred high school girls at a midwest high school, and asked them to read a scenario describing slave day. We then asked the girls to rate the degree to which they were offended on a scale from 1 (inoffensive) to 10 (very offensive.) The average rating for this scenario was 7.7. When asked how they would feel if this activity went on in their school, 31% said they would be angry, 26% said they would be annoyed, and 10% said they would be degraded.

Schools often send the message that females are not as important as males. According to the AAUW report *How Schools Shortchange Girls*, textbooks undervalue and under-represent material on women. When women do appear, their lives are trivialized and distorted. If students are constantly barraged with the message that women's lives count for less than men's lives, the results can be catastrophic. If girls believe themselves capable of less; they will attempt less. If girls are instructed that people like themselves (other women and girls) are less important and not worth studying, we can understand how they adopt a diminished self-concept. Low self-esteem is particularly destructive because a strong self-concept is the very core of achievement.

While girls are learning that they are not as valuable as boys, boys are learning the same lesson. Boys learn that they are more important than girls and come to believe that girls don't have the same rights. They then adopt harassing behaviors.

Harassing behavior serves to identify men as a member of the ruling group to whom the streets and the school hallways belong. Like other forms of sexual violence, sexual harassment is more about power than it is about sex. The astonishing behavior of moaning, jumping, whistling, singing, winking, contorting face and body, hissing obscenities, laughing hysterically and mumbling hoarse endearments to perfect strangers with no apparent provocation are examples of this pattern of intimidation.

This discussion is not intended to be a comprehensive review of sexism in schools or in society. Such a review is far beyond the scope of this book. But we do hope to open some eyes and some hearts to the very real damage done by sex-role stereotyping, sexism, and sexual harassment.

Behavioral Perceptions

Women and men often interpret the same behavior differently. Men tend to perceive interactions that occur in social, business, and academic settings in more sexual terms than do women. According to Catherine Johnson, Margaret Stockdale, and Frank Saal, "When women attempt to create a friendly atmosphere at work or school, that behavior may be interpreted as sexual interest or availability. Men may then act on these misperceptions in a way that is offensive to women and that women label as sexual harassment." According to Frank Saal, Catherine Johnson, and Nancy Weber, "As a woman's behavior becomes more friendly and outgoing when she acclimates to her work or academic environment, men may be quicker to label her behavior as 'sexy' and then to respond in ways the woman construes to be sexually harassing." Other research indicates that men are more likely than women to ascribe responsibility for a sexual harassment incident to the female victim.

In addition to interpreting the same behavior differently, men and women also have different views on the appropriate responses to offensive conduct. Susan Fisk discusses these differences in terms of category-based responses in the human thought and perceptual process. When a man categorizes a female based on her sex, they are evaluating her in terms of characteristics that comport with stereotypes assigned to women rather than in terms of her individual skills or performance. Therefore, if a man categorizes a female along the lines of stereotyped sex-roles, he produces an evaluation of her suitability as a "woman" who might be expected to be sexy, affectionate, and attractive. Females are evaluated less favorably if they do not conform to preconceived stereotypes, regardless of their job performance.

As early as 1978 Margaret Mead attributed the problem of sexual harassment to the socialization process of boys and girls. She believed that parents and teachers were teaching boys to respond to women in inappropriate ways. An example indicating that this attitude persists today can be seen in the following comments made to the authors by the mother of a six-year-old girl.

"My daughter's birthday is right on the cut-off for getting into kindergarten. When I took her to school to ask the teachers and principal for their suggestions regarding enrolling her or holding her out, the male principal said, in front of my daughter, 'I would hold her out. She is pretty small and if you enroll her now her breasts will not be as developed as her classmates when she begins to go to junior high school'."

According to Mead, men treat a woman who has power as someone who has to be cajoled, and a woman without power as someone who can be coerced. Unfortunately, our experience with public schools leads us to believe that Mead's observations are still accurate today.

Differences in Perception

Some of these apparent differences in perception are the result of sexual stereotyping. According to Fiske, there are four preconditions that enhance the presence of stereotyping. These categories are (1) rarity, (2) priming, (3) environment structure, and (4) ambience of the environment.

Rarity exists when an individual's group is smaller in number than its contrasting group so that each individual member is seen as one of a kind. A female student taking a course that has traditionally been identified as a "male course" illustrates the concept of rarity. Because the female student is a clear minority, she is more likely to be harassed by her fellow students and teachers.

Priming means that the educational environment contains objects that encourage stereotypical thinking. Such objects would include photographs of nude and partially nude women, sexual joking, and sexual slurs. If the school environment is contaminated in this way, males will be more likely to view female students as sex objects and interact with them accordingly.

The third precondition for an increased frequency of stereotyping is the nature of the power structure or hierarchy in the school environment. If teachers and administrators tolerate or engage in harassing behavior, students will feel free to sexually harass their fellow students.

And, finally, tolerance of inappropriate conduct promotes the stereotyping of women as sex-objects. The likelihood of stereotyping increases if incidents of complaints of sexual harassment are trivialized. We recently received a phone call from the mother of a high school student. She told us the following story:

> "My daughter, Linda, is in high school. During one of her classes the teacher said, 'Today we are going to talk about the difference between wants and needs. For example, Linda may want me, but she might not need me. Which is it, Linda, do you want me or do you need me?' Many of the students, particularly the boys, laughed.
>
> Linda came home was very upset and told me what happened. I went to the school's principal and told him how upset Linda, her father, and I were about what we thought was inappropriate behavior.
>
> At first the principal said, 'Oh, that's just that teacher's sense of humor. You should not get so upset because I am sure that the teacher did not mean anything by his comments.' When I made it clear that I did not care what the teacher's intentions were, the principal agreed to speak to the teacher.
>
> The next day the teacher began the class by saying, 'Class, I have been told that I must apologize to Linda. It appears that she and her mother don't have much of a sense of humor. I guess we are not going to be able to joke around in here anymore because of Linda.' ""

This incident clearly demonstrates how the educational climate of the school allows sexism and sexual harassment to flourish. If no significant action is taken as a result of female student complaints about graffiti, or language, or photos, the harassing behavior will continue and intensify.

Profile of a Sexual Harasser

Although we run the risk of stereotyping by making generalizations about sexual harassers, there have been several studies that have identified common elements among them. Susan Webb reports that in the workplace, harassers are male, older than their victims, married, and considered unattractive by the victims. Although the most severe harassment is from supervisors to subordinates, the most frequent harassment occurs between co-workers. Webb reports that most harassers bother more that one person and the incidents reoccur over an extended time.

These findings are consistent with the findings of recent surveys of the incidence of sexual harassment in schools. In a survey conducted through *Seventeen* magazine, Nan Stein, Nancy Marshall, and Linda Tropp found that only four percent of the reported incidents of sexual harassment in schools were committed by teachers, counselors, or administrators. Most harassment was committed by fellow students.

According to an AAUW report, *Hostile Hallways*, only 18% of students who reported being sexually harassed say that they were harassed by a school employee such as a teacher, coach, bus driver, teacher's aid, security guard, principal, or counselor. "Of those who say they have been harassed, nearly four in five have been targeted by a current or former student at school. Among girls who have been harassed: 81% report having been harassed by a male acting alone, 57% by a group of males, 11% by a mixed group of males and females, 10% by a female acting alone, and three percent by a group of females." It is interesting to note that the AAUW survey found that of the students that admit to having harassed a fellow student, 94% claim that they themselves have been harassed.

More harassment occurs in environments were there are high percentages of men. This is consistent with our experience that female students are more likely to be harassed in classes or programs that have been traditionally dominated by males.

Profile of a Victim of Sexual Harassment

Webb warns us of generalizing about victims of sexual harassment, but she believes that the following statements can be made. Nine out of ten victims of sexual harassment in the workplace are female. In the workplace most victims are younger than the general female population. Although not a scientific study, the largest number of students that responded to the *Seventeen* study were in the ninth grade. The number of respondents steadily declined in the tenth, eleventh, and twelfth grade. This result is more likely a function of who completed the survey than an indication that older students are not as frequently harassed as younger students.

Chapter Three

Consequences of Sexual Harassment

Extent of the Problem

It is not difficult to find examples of sexual harassment in schools. A shocking, although not unusual, account was reported by Tania Silva in a 1992 article that appeared in the *Gainesville Sun*.

> *"At a school board meeting, a 14-year-old student reported that she could no longer wear a skirt to school. 'The boys pull it up over my hips while others laugh. Now when I wear pants, they back me into a corner and pull them down and start to feel me all over....I'm scared, ashamed, and I feel humiliated.'"*

Ralph Hess reports that sexual harassment in schools ranges from teasing to torment. Boys back girls against walls and make gestures between the girls' legs simulating intercourse, reach under shirts to grab breasts, and force girls to pass through lined-up groups of harassers. As we were writing this section of the book, a father told us this story:

"My daughter came home Friday night and told us what happened to her at school. She said a group of her eighth-grade classmates started chasing her around the room in first hour. They were trying to pull her pants down. She kept running away and trying to get to her seat so that she could sit down. This happened before each class. Finally, before the start of fourth hour they succeeded in pulling her pants and underwear down around her knees. She became so angry that she chased them and hit them with her fists. This took place in the classroom while the teacher was out in the hall. When the teacher came in, he stopped the hitting, found out what happened, and took the boys to the office. When my daughter finished the story she started to cry. She doesn't want to go back to school."

Victims of sexual harassment change their attitudes about school, their classmates, and themselves. Imagine what it must be like to know that you will be threatened, ridiculed, or degraded by your peers. Being the victim of sexual harassment results in a sense of helplessness and lowered self-esteem. According to the National School Safety Center, "In an attempt to escape the harassment, the victim plans activities around an avoidance schedule. Her inability to stop the harassment results in anger, humiliation, and shame. A sense of betrayal and stigmatization often results in isolation and withdrawal from others. Even those few who stand up and fight often lose the battle, thereby reinforcing the feelings of helplessness generated by the abuse."

At a recent workshop which we conducted for a group of teachers and social workers, a male participant commented, "Sexual harassment is really not such a big deal. After all, it's all in fun and no harm is intended." We asked him if he had a daughter. He said he did and began to tell us about how well she was doing in school. We interrupted him and asked if he could bring her to the next session so we could get a look at her tits.

Educators talk about the "teachable moment" as that point in time when the learner is fully ready to grasp the concept. We have never seen a more dramatic "teachable moment." The man's face got red and he looked as if he were going to come out of his chair and throw a punch. Then he simply said, "Oh, I get it!" We apologized to him for our offensive remark. We then used our remark and his response to lead into a discussion about why many men seem to have a difficult time understanding the seriousness of sexual harassment. As long as men see sexual harassment as something that happens to people that they don't know, it is less likely that they will actually "get it."

It seems to us that most women tend to have all of their complex facets and dimensions woven together in an interconnected whole. Many men, on the other hand, seem to be able to divide their lives into a variety of watertight compartments. This idea of compartmentalized life can help explain how a U. S. Senator who has been a leader in the fight for equal rights for women can also be accused of blatant sexual harassment.

If you are a woman, you probably know what it's like to be sexually harassed. If you are a man, you probably have not experienced sexual harassment so, in order to imagine it's effects, ask yourself how you would feel if you knew that your mother, spouse, or daughter was the target of sexual harassment. Consider for a moment how you would feel if your wife faced sexual intimidation on a daily basis while simply trying to do her job. How would you respond if your daughter was forced to run the gauntlet of leers, jeers, and physical sexual abuse as a normal part of her school day?

Although we all wish sexual harassment was not a serious problem, whether we choose to face it or not, sexual harassment is occurring virtually every moment of every day in most every elementary and secondary school in America. Girls are touched, commented upon, and propositioned in the public schools of every city in America. Boys comment on breasts and vaginas and make sexual requests. Some people still believe that girls secretly like this type of attention. Others think that if girls don't like it, they most certainly provoke it with their clothing, their manner of walking, or their behavior. Until recently harassment was recognized as rude, offensive, and impolite, but it was not illegal. However, the rules have changed and sexual harassment in elementary and secondary schools is now against the law.

Occurrence of Sexual Harassment

Recent research indicates that sexual harassment has reached epidemic proportions in our classrooms. It goes on all the time in school - not just teachers harassing students but students harassing students. Sexual harassment is a daily occurrence on school buses and in hallways, in classrooms and laboratories, in gyms and on playing fields. The number of sexual harassment complaints is skyrocketing with a commensurate increase in the number and amount of monetary awards given to compensate victims.

Most sexual harassment in our schools goes unreported. Why would this be so? Why do female students endure the trauma of sexual harassment? Many do not understand what is happening to them. They know that they are made to feel badly. They know that they are being treated differently just because they are girls. But in most cases the school has done nothing to make them believe that their complaints will be taken seriously. Girls often feel that reporting sexual harassment will cause them more embarrassment than enduring the harassment. Many believe that reporting incidents of sexual harassment may result in their being criticized rather than helped with the harassment problem. Young females want to be accepted by males and other females, and if they complain, they assume boys will look upon them as uncooperative, as someone who can't get along. The psychological aspect of sexual harassment is strong. Young women may come to doubt themselves, question the way they handled the situation, or think that they brought the harassment on themselves.

Sexual harassment wreaks havoc on a number of fronts and in a number of different ways. Perhaps the most obviously debilitating manifestation is the physical and emotional harm perpetrated on the victim. The nature and extent of such injuries will be explored in later sections. But there are, in addition to the physical and emotional trauma, other very serious repercussions. One result is that sexual harassment deprives girls and women of equal opportunity. As we'll demonstrate in the following pages, our daughters simply do not have the same educational opportunity as do our sons. Time and time again, sexism and sexual harassment deprive girls of their legal right to an equal education.

Of course, this pattern of discrimination invades the workplace as well. The glass ceiling is real. According to the U.S. Department of Labor's *Glass Ceiling Initiative,* "...the progress of minorities and women in corporate America is affected by more than qualifications....monitoring for equal access and opportunity was almost never considered a corporate responsibility." Tragically, however, the glass ceiling is only one aspect of how women are denied equal employment opportunity. We'll discuss a number of others as we proceed. Finally, sexual harassment does grave damage to our economy. The obvious costs of sexual harassment include legal fees, damages, and loss of productivity. However, there are less apparent but equally expensive ramifications as well. To our knowledge, the true cost of sexual harassment and other conflictual relationships in business has never been measured or even seriously considered. We will attempt to do so.

If you have ever wondered, even for a moment, why you should care about the issue of sexual harassment, the next few pages should be enlightening. For people who wonder why everyone is making such a big deal about sexual harassment, the next few pages might be astonishing. And for those whose heart and mind cries out for justice, the facts you'll read could become a rallying point.

Daughters In Danger

"I've been sexually harassed for almost three years. One guy kept going around the school telling everyone that I gave him head. It made me feel really embarrassed and sad. I didn't know what to do, so I didn't do anything."

14 year old

"My art teacher is constantly telling sick jokes, hugging female students, patting or pinching their butt, looking down their shirts, lifting up skirts, and telling female students how pretty they are. It makes me feel degraded and angry. I told my friends about it, but no one else."

15 year old

"This one guy kept asking me out, making obscene comments and finally would kiss his fingers and wipe them on my mouth. I talked to my friends and finally told the teacher. The boy was moved to a seat farther away from me, but nothing else happened to him."

17 year old

"I asked a teacher to help me with my assignment. He said he couldn't, because he's married. I was bewildered at first and when I realized what he was saying and how he was looking at me I was mad. I dropped out of his class and have not taken any other classes from him."

16 year old

The above comments were written in the Spring of 1993 in response to a questionnaire we distributed in a rural mid-west high school. Even the most callous can recognize the pain and trauma in these words. Please understand, when we talk about sexual harassment in schools, we're talking about real kids and real harm. We're talking about young people whose physical and emotional health is in grave jeopardy. And we are talking about students who feel helpless and hopeless.

Educational Consequences

The AAUW study of sexual harassment in schools was the first to attempt to determine how sexual harassment affects students educationally, emotionally, and behaviorally. The findings of this study clearly indicate that a hostile environment significantly impacts the lives of students. We were particularly chilled and disheartened to learn of the outcome of sexual harassment on female students. This research clearly demonstrates that sexual harassment in our schools is significantly hurting female students' chances for success in school. The most frequent consequence of sexual harassment was to cause the victim to "not want to go to school" (33%). This outcome was followed by; "not wanting to talk as much in class" (32%), "finding it hard to pay attention in school" (28%), "staying home from school or cutting a class" (24%), "making a lower grade on a test paper" (23%), "finding it hard to study" (22%), "making a lower grade in class" (20%), "thinking about changing schools" (18%), and "doubting whether you have what it takes to graduate from high school" (5%). Three percent of the students in this study said that they had actually changed schools as a result of sexual harassment.

Emotional Consequences

According to the AAUW survey, 64% of the female victims of sexual harassment report suffering embarrassment. Similarly, 52% report that sexual harassment has caused them to feel self-conscious, and 43% of the girls report that sexual harassment makes them feel less sure or less confident about themselves. The above findings, alone, should certainly motivate us to work to eliminate sexual harassment from our schools. However, the report goes on to report findings that should motivate us to act quickly and with the knowledge that sexual harassment is having grave consequences on its victims.

Of the girls participating, 39% report that sexual harassment has caused them to feel afraid or scared, and 30% say that sexual harassment has caused them to doubt whether they can have a happy romantic relationship. As we said earlier, boys are also the victims of sexual harassment. However, the AAUW study documents that the consequences of that harassment are not nearly as serious for boys as they are for girls. For example, while 39% of the girls reported feeling afraid or scared, only eight percent of the boys expressed their feelings this way. When students were asked how they felt right after being harassed, 70% of the girls reported being "very upset" or "somewhat upset," compared with only 24% of boys.

When a person is attacked on a consistent basis, and when that person has no effective defense, certain predictable results can occur. As you might expect, the victim often develops a sense of hopelessness. This hopelessness carries potentially grave consequences. Tamara Coder-Mikinski reports on a study that indicates children with a high sense of hopelessness are at greater risk for suicide, depression, and overall psychopathology. A victim of sexual harassment often feels incompetent to deal with the abusive situation. Even more damaging, this feeling of incompetence is often transferred to other life areas. A good student may begin to doubt her ability to deal with the challenges of her education, so her grades fall. Or, she may be unwilling to take the normal risks associated with developing healthy relationships, so she becomes isolated from her friends. When the victims' pleas for help are ignored and she receives no support in her effort to stop the harassment, she may begin to feel that she is unworthy of help, that she deserves the treatment she receives.

These feelings of incompetence and lack of worth are the classic descriptions of low self-esteem and low self-concept. Boys and girls have equal self-esteem between the ages of 7 and 11. However, that soon changes. According to *How Schools Shortchange Girls*, a report published by the American Association of University Women, "by early adolescence, girls self-esteem has fallen significantly compared to boys." The socialization process (including sex-role stereotyping and sexual harassment) has robbed young women of the positive self-image and healthy self-esteem so critical to growth, development, and achievement.

Physical and Psychological Costs

Each person has a subjective perception about themselves that influences how they evaluate their own behavior. It is natural for people to judge themselves in terms of their own worthiness or non-worthiness. Self-esteem is the term used to describe the degree that a person admires or respects or likes themself. People who have high self-esteem view themselves as important, valuable, and worthy of respect. Although these people recognize their own limitations, they believe they will succeed in spite of these limitations.

On the other hand, people with low self-esteem view themselves as unimportant, unlikable, and unworthy of respect. These people don't think that they can control very much in their lives, and consequently they do not think they can achieve success in reaching their goals. Self-esteem is a very strong motivator. There is a consensus among sociologists that self-esteem is the strongest and most important of all sentiments and drives. Kaplan reflects this consensus when he refers to self-esteem as "...universally and characteristically a dominant motive in the individual's motivational system."

To a large extent a person's self-concept and self-esteem is developed during the time that he or she is going to school. According to Coopersmith, in order for children to develop high self-esteem they must receive unconditional acceptance by significant others which is demonstrated by warmth, encouragement, attention, and affection. They must also have the flexibility and freedom to explore within clearly established and enforced limits and rules. High expectations with respect to academic performance, and parental self-esteem are also very important in developing a strong self-concept.

Children are significantly influenced by the attitudes and feedback of significant others, and over the course of time they come to view themselves as they are viewed by others. If a child is rejected and disrespected by her classmates, or if she is discouraged by her parents or teachers, she will develop feelings of inadequacy and worthlessness.

Linda Rubin reports that low self-esteem has been found to significantly correlate with psychiatric assistance, depression, and aggressive behaviors in children. She also found that there is a strong relationship between low self-esteem and anxiety. The symptoms of this anxiety are nervousness, loss of appetite, insomnia, headaches, and reduced task performance.

If female students continue to be short changed in their education, and if schools continue to allow them to be demeaned and harassed by their fellow classmates, it is very likely that they will develop an unstable self-image. Rosenberg believes that people with low self-esteem tend to present "false fronts" as a way to cope with feelings of worthlessness. This is understandable because females receive conflicting messages at school and in the community. On one hand, the media and many parents and educators tell females that they are equal to boys and they can do anything they want to do with their lives. On the other hand, sexual harassment makes many females feel unsure of themselves and out of control.

Rosenberg has shown that social classification based on sex can profoundly effect a person's sense of identity. If female students attend a school where any ride on a school bus or walk down the hall can result in being insulted and humiliated, their self-esteem will be significantly and negatively impacted.

Common complaints resulting from sexual harassment include headaches and ulcers. When a female student is sexually harassed and nothing is done to stop the harassment, more serious stress-related diseases can develop. A student under very high stress may become unable to function normally.

But there is even more. There is fear, anger, and depression. Research indicates that women suffer twice as many depressive disorders as men. While we can't attribute the incidence of these depressive disorders solely to sexual harassment, we strongly believe there is a significant correlation, particularly with regard to adolescent females. It should not surprise us that a young woman faced with unrelenting abuse might find the circumstances of her life quite depressing. And depression is significantly associated with suicide and suicide attempts. Virtually all studies of suicide include depression as a contributing factor to suicide attempts or as a predominant personality characteristic of the victim. It is also illuminating that females attempt suicide three times more often than do males.

The other predictable response to harassment without respite is anger and hostility. In a thought provoking book entitled *Anger Kills*, authors Redford and Virginia Williams present a compelling case that "Anger is a toxin to your body." Their research documents a significant correlation between hostility and very serious health concerns. For example, the incidence of coronary heart disease and cancer is substantially increased in people who are assessed as highly hostile. There are also indications that hostility negatively affects the immune system. And according Williams and Williams, hostile people are also "...more likely to be smokers, to consume more alcohol and to have a larger body and mass index (a measure of obesity.)" They summarize their findings by saying, "hostility is a personality trait that exerts a most deleterious effect on physical health." It is clear, the physical and emotional carnage of sexual harassment is immense.

Behavioral Consequences

Although they were discussing sexual discrimination on college campuses (rather than in elementary and secondary schools) when they made the comment, Roberta Hall and Bernice Sandler found classrooms to have a "chilly" climate for women. According to them, "Whether overt or subtle, differential treatment based on sex is far from innocuous. Its cumulative effects can be damaging not only to individual women and men students but also to the educational process." Female students are put at a significant disadvantage if they are forced to attempt to learn in a chilling classroom climate. According to Hall and Sandler, this type of climate has a profound negative impact on females' academic and career development by:

√ discouraging classroom participation;
√ preventing students from seeking help outside of class;
√ causing students to drop or avoid certain classes, to switch major or subspecialities within majors, and in some instances even to leave a given institution;
√ minimizing the development of individual collegial relationships with faculty which are crucial for future professional development.
√ dampening career aspirations; and

√   undermining confidence.

A chilly climate may also result in causing women to believe and act as though:

√   their presence in a given class, department, program or institution is at best peripheral, or at worst an unwelcome intrusion;

√   their participation in class discussion is not expected, and their contributions are not important;

√   their capacity for full intellectual development and professional success is limited; and

√   their academic and career goals are not matters for serious attention or concern.

Although women students are the most directly harmed by an inhospitable climate, Hall and Sandler believe that male students are also affected. "If limited views of women are overtly or subtly communicated by faculty, some men students may experience reinforcement of their own negative views about women especially because such views are confirmed by persons of knowledge and status. This will result in men having a difficult time seeing women as full peers to work with, collaborate with, and support as colleagues.

The AAUW study on sexual harassment in our schools documents the following additional behavioral consequences for victims of sexual harassment; avoiding the person(s) who harassed them, staying away from particular places in the school or on the school grounds, changing their seats in class, stopping attending a particular activity or sport, changing their group of friends, and changing the way they come to or go home from school.

There Is No Such Thing As Equal Opportunity. Yet.

Sexual harassment that causes the serious health issues we have been discussing also deprives girls of the opportunity for a fair and equitable education. This occurs in a number of different ways. Sometimes girls simply can't face the torture any longer, and they leave school completely. In these cases, sexual harassment deprives the victim of not only an equal education, but of any education at all. Often, however, girls who are harassed attempt to escape the harassment by abandoning certain classes or fields of study. An extreme example of the consequences of sexual harassment of a female in a non-traditional class is seen in the following report:

> *Kelly is a student in the auto body repair class. Her teacher told her to move a 100 lb. box of parts. She wanted to prove that she could do it. She knew that all the boys were watching her. After several failed attempts she gave one more try. She ripped open her intestines and was rushed to the hospital. After surgery and an extensive recovery period she learned that none of the boys would have lifted that box.*

Sexual harassment can be a significant deterrent for girls to enroll in non-traditional programs. Is it fair that any student should be so intimidated that she feels compelled to leave a class or subject? How can educational opportunity ever be equal for boys and girls when certain classes are off limits to girls? The answer, of course, is that as long as sexual harassment exists in our schools, equal educational opportunity for girls will never be achieved.

There are additional, more subtle ways in which sexual harassment and other forms of sexual discrimination deny female children the opportunity for an equal education. Most of these stem from sex-role stereotyping and other sexist notions so prevalent in our society. For example, teachers routinely give more attention to boys than to girls in the classroom setting. In January of 1993, *Twins* magazine reported on research conducted by Myra and David Sadker. Their research revealed startling evidence of classroom gender bias. According to Myra Sadker, "Teachers give boys more attention than girls. Boys get more constructive help and are asked more probing questions to help them get the answers. Praise for appearance was the only area we found girls got more attention. We also found that boys got more criticism, which when handled well can be very helpful to children." When researchers asked why (boys got more criticism) teachers said they were afraid girls would cry. The unfortunate upshot is that girls never get a chance to learn how to handle criticism. Other research indicates that teachers treat boys more seriously and validate their thoughts more frequently. This perverted "girls education" is clearly illustrated by the following cartoon.

Doonesbury   BY GARRY TRUDEAU

These and other destructive influences have the effect of discouraging girls from pursuing certain endeavors, and limiting their achievement when they do. While elementary school girls consistently score equal to boys in standardized testing for math, by the time the students reach middle school, boys have forged ahead. We have no evidence to suggest that the disparity in achievement comes from anything other than gender bias, in the classroom and in society.

Society's impact in and out of the classroom is dramatic. Consider the influence of television. According to the A.C. Nielsen ratings company, kids watch an average of 20 hours of television every week. Given the time children spend with TV, as well as the cultural power of the medium, a case can be made for television being a very significant determinant of children's attitudes and values. And what do kids learn from television? Unfortunately, they often learn that little girls aren't quite as important as little boys. According to Peggy Charren, president and founder of Action for Children's Television, "The heroes on children's network television are almost without exception male. And when there are two heroes, there are two males; when there are 99 heroes, there are 99 males."

When society's message that girls aren't really as competent as boys is reinforced in school, it is extraordinarily difficult for a female student to embrace any other view. When everyone and everything in a little girl's life tells her she's not quite as capable or worthy as a boy, it is easy to understand why she tends believe it. This insidious undermining of female self-concept decimates any chance for an equal educational opportunity.

Economic Consequences of Sexual Harassment

The price we pay for sexual harassment is high. Sexual harassment results in economic, physical, psychological, and educational loss. There is certainly no way to place a dollar cost on the kind of damage done to the physical and emotional health of the victims of sexual harassment and sexism. At the same time, it seems almost immoral to discuss the economic loss involved when we rob our daughters of dignity, opportunity, and respect. However, to ignore the costs and economic ramifications would be to ignore reality. And if we ignore the costs, we might miss an opportunity to demonstrate the need for change.

Sexual harassment is expensive. It costs companies, citizens, and school districts millions of dollars every day. The Merit Systems Protection Board survey estimated the economic cost of sexual harassment in 1988 to be over $267,000,000. Some estimates now place the annual cost of sexual harassment over two billion dollars. Direct costs of sexual harassment include legal fees and awards for damages, job turnover, sick leave, and other medical expenses as well as loss of morale and productivity.

However, these estimates consider only the costs of sexual harassment according to the legal definition. The estimates do not take into account our broader perspective of sexual harassment as a flashpoint in the continuum of contentious relations between men and women. If we include the costs incurred as a result of conflictual relationships between men and women, the magnitude of our loss is truly staggering.

Most every adult who has been involved in a significant relationship with a member of the other sex has, at one time or another, experienced conflict in that relationship. People know what contentious relations are all about, because most everyone has been there. Has the turmoil in your relationship ever negatively affected your work? Have you ever been less than 100% effective because your heart and your mind have been otherwise occupied? Have you ever been so angry, frustrated or upset that you could barely get through the day? Most of us can answer yes to at least one of these questions. And, truth be told, many of us could probably answer yes to all of them.

Now we get to a critical question. How much does our loss of productivity cost? We really don't know, but we would like for you to go along with us for a moment. If we assume the average person has a net loss of one work day (eight hours) per year as a result of conflict in an important relationship with a member of the other sex, we believe we have estimated conservatively. That loss represents approximately one half of one percent (.005) of the total investment in an employee. If the total cost for a single employee was $30,000, the yearly loss attendant to conflictual relationships would be about $150. Maybe that doesn't sound like a big deal. But, when we consider that the payroll in this country is about $3.6 trillion per year, the productivity lost to contentious relationships carries a price tag of about $18 billion.

But those calculations (as flawed as they may be) only take into account the cost of conflictual relations with a significant other. What if, on the average, we each lose another day of productivity every year as a result of bickering and feuding with another member of the other sex? Here, we are asking you to consider primarily the conflicts you encounter at work. We hope by this point you have come to recognize that many of the disputes in which you are involved, and many of the stressful situations that occur, result from the underlying conflict between men and women. With these thoughts in mind, we can reasonably suggest that the true cost of sexual harassment and the conflictual relations between men and women approaches the $36 billion level every year. $36,000,000,000 would pay our defense bill for a month or reduce our national budget deficit by almost 10%.

Obviously, we're not economists. And, we don't mean to suggest that the numbers we've bandied about are necessarily precise. However, we are convinced that they should be taken seriously. Sexual harassment is devastating. It damages people, it destroys careers, and it costs millions of dollars every day.

Chapter Four

Sexual Harassment and The Law

The Function of Laws and Courts

Because most of us want a harmonious society, we voluntarily allow laws to regulate our behavior. Lawmakers and judges are involved in the constant process of attempting to strike a balance that allows individuals as much freedom as possible while at the same time protecting the rights of others. The Constitution protects our individual rights while various state and federal laws protect the general welfare of society and implement the constitutional protection of individuals.

Laws are not made in isolation from what is happening in society. As society changes and new relationships evolve, new laws are needed to respond to the new view of what is right and what is wrong. As groups of people request or demand legal protection, public opinion interacts with lawmaking to ensure that new laws reflect the values of the majority. Consequently, laws both shape and reflect the values of society.

Because our society is made up of people who hold many different values, new rules are not accepted by everyone at the same rate. Some people are way out in front of a value shift. They are the people who are fighting for a new idea before most of us understand what they are talking about. For example, Farley coined the term sexual harassment in 1974, but it wasn't until 1986 that the Supreme Court ruled that sexual harassment was a form of sex discrimination. By the time a new idea is formalized into law, most people have formed an opinion about it, and the majority of the people accept the new law. However, there are always people who continue to fight against a new value, even after it is passed into law. They keep testing the resolve of society to uphold the new law. Some of this testing takes place in private actions and some takes place in the courts.

The current confusion about the legal status of sexual harassment is an example of the complex process of translating a new value into new rules for behavior. While some people are fighting to gain equal treatment for women, others are resisting any change in the role and status of women. When there are conflicting beliefs about appropriate and inappropriate behavior, courts are asked to resolve the controversy. The process is further confused by the fact that judges, as part of society, have their own sets of values. Therefore, each judge interprets the law through his or her own set of values.

Laws are society's attempt to ensure that consequences will result if certain prohibited acts are committed. Courts were created to interpret the laws and to ensure that all citizens are treated equally and judged by the same standards of behavior when consequences are meted out. The overall purpose of laws and the court system is to produce solidarity, continuity, and conformity within society. The end result of all law is justice.

Because no law can specifically describe all possible actions, we don't know exactly which specific behaviors are legal and which are illegal until a court makes a ruling on the specific facts of a case. Therefore, the court system has a major influence on all of our behavior. As our attitudes toward women have evolved, courts have been called upon to provide clarification regarding women's legal rights. For a long time courts reinforced society's paternalistic belief that "a woman's place was in the home." By looking at a few of these court decisions we will be able to see that there has been a gradual shift in the courts' view of women.

One of the most famous cases which illustrates a paternalistic view of women is the 1872 case of *Bradwell v. Illinois*. In this decision the U.S. Supreme Court upheld the Illinois Supreme Court's refusal to allow women to practice law. In his concurring opinion Justice Bradley wrote, "Man is or should be woman's protector and defender...the natural and proper timidity and delicacy which belong to the female sex evidently unfits it for many of the occupations of civil life...the paramount destiny and mission of women are to fulfill the noble and benign offices of wife and mother."

Thirty years later, in the case of *Muller v. Oregon*, the U. S. Supreme Court affirmed a decision that restricted the number of hours that a woman could work during any one day on the grounds that "...history discloses the fact that woman has always been dependent upon man...it cannot be denied that she still looks to her brother and depends upon him. The reason rests on the inherent difference between the two sexes, and in the different functions in life which they perform."

As recently as 1966, in the case of *State v. Hall,* a Mississippi court upheld a state statute that excluded women from serving on juries. The court stated that women should be excluded so that "they may continue their service as mothers, wives, and homemakers, and so to protect them from the filth, obscenity, and obnoxious atmosphere that so often pervades a courtroom during a jury trial."

In a 1973 case that involved secondary school students, a state court ruled that girls could be excluded from a high school cross-country running team because, "Athletic competition builds character in boys. We don't need that kind of character in our girls, the women of tomorrow."

Sexual Harassment is Against the Law

In the late 1960s and early 1970s concerned teachers, students and parents began to struggle against sex bias and discrimination in our nations schools. This awareness and commitment resulted in the passage of Title IX of the Education Amendments of 1972.

It has only been in the last decade that courts have clearly placed women under the protection of the U.S. Constitution. Although it is now well established that sexual harassment is sexual discrimination, this understanding is still evolving. The definition of sexual harassment not only changes from situation to situation, but from case to case, and from court to court.

The earliest sexual harassment cases came from events that took place in the workplace, later cases emerged from colleges and universities, and recently many sexual harassment cases are originating in elementary and secondary schools.

Lower courts and the U. S. Supreme Court are gradually clarifying the legal status of sexual harassment. Each new case provides more clarity as to what constitutes sexual harassment. As a result of court action, the Equal Employment Opportunity Commission regulations on sexual harassment have been upheld as a lawful regulatory interpretation of Title VII of the Civil Rights Act of 1964, and that sexual harassment is a violation of Title IX of the Education Amendments of 1972.

As a direct result of the Senate confirmation hearings of Judge Clarence Thomas, Congress enacted the Civil Rights Act of 1991 for the express purpose of providing "additional remedies under federal law...to deter unlawful harassment." By providing for compensatory and punitive damages relating to punishment and providing a trial by jury, this act actually encourages suits charging sexual harassment. In addition to the back pay, front pay, reinstatement, and attorneys' fees previously available under Title VII, this act authorizes as much as $300,000 in compensatory damages.

The law regarding sexual harassment of students in less clear than harassment of adults for several reasons. Problems arise because most of the victims and harassers are minors, and our legal system has a difficult time evaluating both harm and responsibility when minors are involved. Although she was referring to college students when she made the following comments, Laurie LeClair's comments are also relevant to elementary and secondary school students. She identifies three factors that add to the courts' confusion. They are (1) students are more likely than employees to be transient, and consequently their interest in institutional reform tends to be short lived, (2) students lack financial incentives to pursue litigation, and (3) courts are more reluctant to intervene in the academic context than in the non-academic context.

The laws that govern sexual harassment of elementary and secondary school teachers are the same as those that affect all public, federally funded entities. For example, whether you are an office worker or a fourth grade teacher, you are protected from discrimination by Title VII of the Civil Rights Act and section 1983 of the United States Code. This law is enforced by the Equal Employment Opportunity Commission (EEOC), a federal agency.

Public school students are protected by Title IX of the Education Amendments of 1972. Title IX is one of the most sweeping sex discrimination laws ever passed. Although it had little early enforcement, it is now the primary tool that defines equal educational opportunity for women in schools. Under Title IX, sexual harassment is defined as *"verbal or physical conduct of a sexual nature, imposed on the basis of sex, by an employee or agent of a recipient that denies, limits, provides different, or conditions the provision of aid, benefits, services or treatment protected under Title IX."*

In addition to criminal charges (assault, battery, rape, etc.), because sexual harassment often involves unsolicited, offensive, physical touching and psychological and emotional harm, victims of sexual harassment can bring additional state law civil claims against the harasser. This type of claim for redress of a civil wrong is known as a tort. These tort claims include assault, battery, and intentional infliction of emotional distress.

Sexual Harassment Continuum

As we look at the various behaviors on this continuum we must remember that in order for any of these behaviors to be considered sexual harassment they must be unwanted. We can also see that as we move to the right on the continuum the behaviors become progressively more serious. At the left of the continuum are behaviors that must occur frequently and persistently in order for them to be strictly considered as sexual harassment. However, as we move to the right the behaviors become more severe. Just one incident at the right half of the continuum would probably be considered sexual harassment. For example, staring at a woman's breasts, vaginal area or buttocks is clearly rude. However, it must occur persistently and flagrantly to be considered sexual harassment. On the other hand, even one incident of solicitation of sexual activity by a teacher is sexual harassment. And any unwanted physical touching or physical assault is considered sexual harassment as well as a violation of other statutory protections.

In addition to federal protection, most states have civil rights statutes which govern discrimination, including sexual harassment. Some state civil rights statutes have general prohibitions against sexual discrimination. However, states such as Connecticut specifically define sexual harassment as a "discriminatory employment practice." Although most of the current law relating to sexual harassment developed from cases where the victims of the harassment were adults, more recent cases involve elementary and secondary school students. California, Illinois, Iowa, Minnesota, and Wisconsin have statutes that specifically prohibit sexual harassment in schools. For example, all Minnesota schools are currently required to have written sexual harassment policies. These policies must include rules and consequences that are posted in the schools and included in student handbooks. All athletic and extra-curricular programs must have a specific policy against sexual harassment and violence.

In 1993 Minnesota Attorney General Hubert Humphrey III conducted a state wide survey to determine the impact and level of compliance with the Minnesota sexual harassment statute. The results of the survey are discouraging. According to Humphrey, "While all responding schools said they have developed written policies, only 38% believe their policy is well understood by students and staff." Humphrey believes that training and education are essential to ensure that students and staff clearly understand what harassment is, who to report to, and what the consequences are. It is interesting to note that although the survey was completed by superintendents, principals or guidance counselors, 12% didn't know if their students were required to attend the training sessions. On the next page is a chart that shows how sexual harassment in elementary and secondary schools occurs on a continuum, ranging from environmental to *quid pro quo* to physical force.

Sexual Harassment Continuum

ENVIRONMENTAL VISUAL	ENVIRONMENTAL WRITTEN	ENVIRONMENTAL VERBAL	ENVIRONMENTAL PHYSICAL	QUID PRO QUO VERBAL	PHYSICAL FORCE
•Staring	•Magazines	•Sexual innuendoes	•Standing "too close"	•Pressure for dates	•Physical corrosion for sex
•Ogling	•Flyers	•Using sexist, derogatory language	•Brushing against	•Pressure for sex	•Physical assault
•Obscene gestures	•Graffiti	•Unwanted requests for dates	•Touching	•Unwanted phone calls	•Rape
•Mooning	•Cartoons	•Lewd comments	•Patting	•Implied threats of retaliation	
•Simulating masturbation	•Photos	•Insulting sounds	•Grabbing	•Overt threats of retaliation	
•Simulating intercourse	•Posters	•"Dirty"/sexual jokes	•Pinching		
	•Obscene fax messages	•Questions about personal life	•Caressing		
	•Obscene e-mail	•Comments about body	•Kissing		
	•Obscene poems	•Spreading rumors	•Touching hair		
	•Unwanted notes		•Fondling		
	•Unwanted letters		•"Flipping" skirt up		
			•Stalking		
			•Coerced sex		

© 1993 Shoop and Hayhow, used by permission.

What is Sexual Harassment?

Over the past ten years most sexual harassment cases have been based upon the *EEOC Guidelines on Discrimination Because of Sex*. According to these guidelines, unwelcome sexual advances, requests for sexual favors, and other verbal or physical conduct of a sexual nature is sexual harassment if; (1) submission to such conduct is made either explicitly or implicitly a term or condition of an individual's employment, (2) submission to or rejection of such conduct by an individual is used as the basis for employment decisions affecting such individual, or (3) such conduct has the purpose or effect of unreasonably interfering with an individual's work performance or creating an intimidating, hostile, or offensive working environment. The first two subsections of the EEOC guidelines define *quid pro quo* harassment. The third subsection describes environmental sexual harassment. A subset of the hostile work environment is known as sexual favoritism.

Quid pro quo, environmental, and sexual favoritism sexual harassment regularly occur in our elementary and secondary schools. Although it is sometimes difficult to distinguish between the categories, it is important to do so because school districts are held to different standards for each.

Sexual activity between two consenting adults is not illegal in the workplace. Such sexual activity is not sexual harassment unless it is unwanted. However, sexual activity between an adult and a minor student is always illegal. Sexual activity between a teacher and a student, or propositions for such activity are grounds for dismissal and for criminal action against the teacher.

Because of the special relationship between the school and the student, schools have a duty to protect students from sexual abuse by teachers. In addition to violating criminal law, a teacher having sex with a student is also a form of *quid pro quo* sexual harassment. Because this type of behavior is covered by criminal law, we will not discuss it in detail, other than to say that schools are liable for *quid pro quo* harassment regardless of whether or not the school knew about the harassment.

Whether it takes place in the workplace or the school, environmental sexual harassment is not as easy to identify. Therefore, schools are usually liable only if the school knew or should have known of the harassment and did not take adequate steps to prevent it.

Just as most parents are not aware that their daughters are being sexually harassed in school, many teachers and administrators are also unaware of the extent of the problem. This does not mean that they do not see the behavior, they simply do not recognize that it is illegal. Boys have been behaving inappropriately toward girls for so long that it is often accepted as the norm. The following two events were reported to us this year by elementary school teachers.

> *"During recess at an elementary school two or three boys pick out one girl they really like. The boys chase the girl, catch her, and each boy takes a turn giving the 'girl of his dreams' a kiss on her mouth."*

> *"During recess boys pick out one girl and chase after her. After catching her, one of the boys pulls down her pants. Then all the boys run away and start after another girl."*

If you think back to your own elementary school days, you can probably remember an event similar to one of the above. You might have even participated in such an activity. Does the event bring a smile to your face or does it bring memories of pain? We recently asked a group of high school girls to tell us about incidents from their past that they now thought might have been examples of sexual harassment. One girl quietly said, "Please don't ask me to talk about this. It makes me too sad." Before you discount her reaction as being overly sensitive, ask yourself how you react to the following story, told to us by the parent of the girl involved.

> *"My daughter attended a high school football game with a group of girl friends. As she was coming back from the bathroom a group of boys jumped her and pulled her to the ground. They pulled her sweatshirt and bra up around her neck and wrote their names on her chest with magic markers. What really hurt her the most was that these boys were her friends. They said they were 'just fooling around.'"*

Regardless of how you remember your school days, or how you personally react to the above stories, today each of these events are examples of sexual harassment. Clearly, the rules have changed. What may have been acceptable behavior even a short time ago is now considered sexual harassment. Many teachers and administrators are not aware of this change and they do not understand that they are responsible for seeing that sexual harassment does not take place in their schools. Consequently most schools have done little or nothing to stop sexual harassment of students.

Just as 1986 is remembered as the year that the U. S. Supreme Court ruled sexual harassment is an illegal form of sex discrimination, 1992 will be remembered as the year when educators were informed that sexual harassment of students is also an illegal form of sex discrimination. The U. S. Supreme Court made it clear that schools owe their students protection from sexual harassment by teachers and by other students.

Schools must act in a pro-active manner to eradicate sexual harassment. Whether subtle or overt, sexual harassment is categorized as either *quid pro quo*, sexual favoritism, or hostile educational environment. However, many educators still do not recognize or understand the extent or seriousness of the problem. Let's look at the three categories of sexual harassment in the context of a school environment.

Quid Pro Quo

Quid pro quo sexual harassment is the easiest type of harassment to recognize. It occurs when sexual demands are made upon a student in exchange for educational participation, advancement, or other benefits. Even one such incident is *quid pro quo* sexual harassment. Because of the age and vulnerability of students, even if the female student "welcomes" the sexual attention, the school is liable for sexual harassment and the offending teacher is liable for sexual harassment as well as other criminal charges.

Although *quid pro quo* harassment is clearly a violation of Title IX, some courts have drawn a distinction between standard and retaliatory *quid pro quo*. Standard *quid pro quo* harassment involves expressed or implied demands for sexual favors in return for some benefit, such as a grade, special treatment, or a letter of reference. Retaliatory *quid pro quo* exists when a teacher makes sexual advances to a student without either expressing or implying that the student will be affected by a refusal. It becomes sexual harassment if, upon being refused, the teacher then makes life miserable for the student. The distinction between standard and retaliatory *quid pro quo* is usually not significant because both categories are classified as sexual harassment.

Sexual Favoritism

Sexual favoritism is also fairly easy to identify. It occurs when a student receives benefits as a result of his or her submission to the teacher's sexual advances or requests for sexual favors. The victims of the harassment are the other students in the class who are treated unfairly because they are not objects of the teacher's romantic interest. In the workplace, this type of sexual harassment has resulted in successful law suits brought on behalf of qualified persons who were denied employment opportunities or benefits. However, courts have required proof of the sexual relationship, not merely rumors or innuendos. Courts have yet to offer consistent views on how to treat sexual harassment cases in which a student is favored by a teacher who has a romantic interest in her.

Hostile Learning Environment

In the workplace this is called hostile work environment sexual harassment, in a school setting we will call this a hostile learning environment. Hostile learning environment is the form of sexual harassment that is the most confusing to many people. This form of harassment is less tangible, less discrete, and often occurs over a period of time. Unlike *quid pro quo* and sexual favoritism harassment, which may involve a single incident, sexually hostile or intimidating environments are characterized by multiple, varied, and frequent occurrences.

What Constitutes A Hostile Learning Environment?

In the school setting the hostile environment theory is based on the assumption that the relationship between the student and the school is very significant and that students should be protected from psychological as well as physical abuse. Each student should be able to come to school free from fear and free from harm.

In a case where an elementary school girl complained to the school after an elementary school boy used extremely graphic and abusive sexual language on the school bus, the school principal and several parents said that the boy's behavior was inappropriate, but that it was not sexual harassment. They argued that in order for sexual harassment to exist the offending student must have a sophisticated understanding of sexuality, and must have intended the behavior to be sexual. This argument demonstrates a lack of understanding of sexual harassment. The *intent* of the harasser is irrelevant. It is the *impact* of the action that determines whether or not sexual harassment has taken place.

In order for a behavior to be considered to have created a hostile environment, four elements must exist. First, the harassment must be based on a person's sex. (It will be unlikely that a court will find behavior that is equally offensive to men and women to be sexual harassment.) This does not mean that a school cannot prohibit such behavior, but a victim will probably not succeed in a sexual harassment suit. Second, the sexual behavior must be unwelcome to the victim. The victim must not have solicited or incited the offensive behavior, and the victim must regard the conduct as undesirable or offensive. If a female student engages in sexual banter and frequently uses sexual innuendos, she may have a difficult time convincing a judge that later, more offensive behavior is sexual harassment. Third, the offensive behavior must be sufficiently severe or pervasive to alter conditions of the school climate and create a hostile learning environment. One off-color joke or comment will usually not be considered to be sexual harassment. And fourth, in order for the school to be liable for sexual harassment, the school district must have known or should have known of the harassment and failed to take prompt, effective, remedial action. Because the school district is expected to control the educational environment, it is held responsible for sexual harassment.

Some people are confused about the hostile learning environment in schools, because in many cases the harasser is a student who has no formal, recognized authority over the victim. Secondly, because student victims of sexual harassment often have no obvious loss or physical injury, some people do not recognize that an injury has occurred. And finally, much of the behavior that female students find offensive is behavior that has long been accepted as normal heterosexual behavior by many men and boys. It must be remembered that schools are liable for sexual harassment if the behavior creates an intimidating, offensive or hostile environment regardless of any other impact on the students.

Harassment by A Fellow Student

In the *Meritor* decision, the U.S. Supreme Court ruled that sexual harassment violates Title VII if it creates a hostile or offensive environment for the victim, regardless of whether it threatened the individual's job. Although the *Meritor* decision was based on Title VII, Title IX cases will likely follow the same judicial reasoning. In the school setting, this means that student initiated unwelcome sexual advances, requests for sexual favors, and other verbal or physical conduct of a sexual nature constitute sexual harassment. A key question is whether the sexual advances were unwelcome.

Remarks that simply offend a person's feelings are usually not sexual harassment. However, if the offending behavior is severe or pervasive enough to actually affect a student's learning environment, then it is sexual harassment. In this context there is a clear difference between welcome and voluntary. For example, even if an alleged victim agreed to participate in sexual intimacy, the sexual advances are a prohibited form of sexual harassment if it is clear that the victim did not desire to have the sexual relationship, but capitulated under pressure.

The Concept of Welcomeness

Because the 1980 EEOC guidelines do not define "unwelcome," we must look to various court cases in order to understand the difference between a voluntary activity and a welcome activity. In the *Meritor* case the victim claimed that she initially refused the sexual advances of her supervisor, but she eventually gave in and engaged in sexual intercourse out of fear of losing her job. The Supreme Court ruled that her participation in a sexual relationship did not establish that the relationship was truly consensual or welcome. The Court ruled that "the fact that the sex-related conduct was voluntary, in the sense that the complainant was not forced to participate against her will, is not a defense to a sexual harassment suit brought under Title VII." The court in the 1982 case of *Henson v. City of Dundee*, provided a general definition of welcomeness that has been followed by many other courts. Challenged conduct must be unwelcome "in the sense that the employee did not solicit or incite it, and in the sense that the employee regarded the conduct as undesirable or offensive."

In 1990 the EEOC issued its *Policy Guidance on Current Issues of Sexual Harassment.* These guidelines instructed that when there is conflicting evidence of welcomeness, "the record as a whole and the totality of the circumstances," should be used to evaluate on a case by case basis. EEOC suggests that if there is a complaint of unwelcome sexual attention, the complaint is strengthened if it is made immediately after the event.

Severe or Pervasive

How much sexual harassment must a student endure before she has a case that will hold up in court? The EEOC has consistently ruled that "sexual flirtation or innuendo, even vulgar language that is trivial or merely annoying, will not usually be considered a violation of law." For example, if a male student calls a female student a "bitch" after a disagreement, it may be rude, it may be inappropriate, but it is probably not sexual harassment. Although probably not sexual harassment, this does not mean that a school should approve or permit such offensive behavior. However, if the above mentioned boy follows the girl down the hall shouting obscenities at her, writes vulgar comments about her on the bathroom walls, and spreads sexual rumors about her, then the behavior is then sufficiently pervasive and severe to qualify as sexual harassment.

Reasonableness

Courts will find a person liable for sexual harassment if the actions are unwelcome, and if there is a pattern of severe or pervasive behavior. In light of the above discussion, it is logical to ask, "What standard does the court use to make this determination?" Until recently, the basis for finding that a behavior is sufficiently severe or pervasive to constitute sexual harassment was the objective standard of "reasonableness." Historically this test question asked whether a "reasonable person," under the victim's circumstances, would consider the action to be hostile. Early courts looked at the behavior to determine if it "would have interfered with a reasonable individual's work performance."

Although the EEOC's guidelines support the reasonable person test, recent court decisions indicate that courts are becoming aware of the gender hierarchy that shapes much of the interaction between women and men in the workplace and at school. That is, women and men often interpret the same behavior differently.

Circuit Judge Beezer stated that if the reasonable person standards were accepted, victims of sexual harassment would have to endure the harassment until their psychological well-being was seriously affected to the extent that they suffered anxiety and debilitation before they could establish a hostile environment. He said that sexual harassment falls somewhere between forcible rape and the mere utterance of an epithet. "Although an isolated epithet by itself fails to support a cause of action for a hostile environment, Title VII's protection of employees from sex discrimination should come into play long before the point where victims of sexual harassment require psychiatric assistance."

The danger in using the reasonable person test when it is clear that boys and girls see the same situation differently can be illustrated by listening to how some boys view sexual harassment. When asked to view video taped scenes of various forms of sexual harassment, boys often recognize that the girl in the scene is offended by the behavior, but they make comments such as "That's just the way boys are," or "I don't see the problem, the boys were just joking," or "if the girls don't like the way boys talk or behave they should not go into classes or jobs that are 'men's' work."

In evaluating a hostile work environment, the focus should be on the perspective of the victim. Using the "reasonable person" standard runs the risk of reinforcing the prevailing level of discrimination (i.e., if men and women see things differently, and courts continued to use the reasonable man test, then it would be unlikely that women would win many sexual harassment cases.) Men and boys could continue to harass merely because a particular discriminatory practice was common, and women and girls would have no remedy. There is a broad range of view-points among women as a group, of course, but many women share common concerns which men do not. A "reasonable person" standard tends to be male-biased and ignores the experiences of women.

Beezer states that "by acknowledging and not trivializing the effects of sexual harassment on a 'reasonable woman,' courts can work towards ensuring that neither men nor women will have to 'run a gauntlet of sexual abuse' in return for the privilege of being allowed to work and make a living."

Courts have held that "the objective standard asks whether a reasonable person of the same sex as the victim, that is, a reasonable woman, would perceive that an abusive working environment has been created." In schools this means that the concept of psychological well-being is measured by the impact of the school environment on a "reasonable female" student's school performance or more broadly by the impact of the stress inflicted on her by the continuing presence of the harassing behavior. The fact that some female students do not complain of the school environment or find some behaviors objectionable does not mean that the school environment as a whole is not offensive.

In light of the above discussion, one point must be clarified. Just because men and women may interpret each others behaviors differently, it does not mean that intimidating, hostile or offensive school environments are simply the result of differences of perceptions. In the *Sparks* case, the court stated that "the whole point of sexual harassment claims is that behavior that may be permissible in some settings can be abusive in the workplace." This means that behavior that may occur in a person's home or in his or her social life is not sexual harassment, regardless of how rude or offensive it is. However, that same behavior on a school bus or in the school building may be grounds for charges of sexual harassment.

Sexual Harassment of Males and Homosexuals

Throughout our discussion we have focused on the sexual harassment of female students by male faculty members and students. As we stated earlier, we did this because the impact of sexual harassment is greater on females than it is on males. However, it must be acknowledged that boys as well as girls can be the victims of sexual harassment at school. According to Pat Mahony, boys are more likely to suffer sexual harassment if they do not conform to male stereotypes. Because of the apparent contempt that many boys hold for girls, boys emphasize their masculinity to prove that they are as unlike girls as possible. In fact, boys often use girls as their negative reference group. Mahony believes that in order to escape sexual harassment themselves, boys are pressured to adopt the sexual predatory behavior of their peers.

Mahony recounts a rather bizarre experiment conducted by a male teacher to determine whether his students were *normal*. In front of an all male class the teacher suddenly announced, "There's a naked woman running across the playground." All but one boy rushed to the window. As the boys were returning to their seats, the single boy who had remained seated objected to the experiment as sexist. The teacher announced to the class, "Now we know who isn't normal." Mahony reports that the teacher and class ridiculed the student and the other students physically abused him outside the classroom. Hopefully this is not an example of typical teacher or student behavior. However, it does indicate how being perceived as different and feminine can result in harassment. Because sexual harassment is often a group activity, boys often feel pressure to go along with the harassment, in order to belong. The National School Safety Counsel argues, "In most cases, the identity of the victims is unimportant since the purpose of the activity is to prove masculinity. Many accounts of sexual harassment report strong peer support as evidenced by cheering and egging the offenders on." Clearly, policies must be written so that individuals are held accountable for their own actions.

Title VII protects men and women from being harassed by homosexuals because such harassment is based on gender. Another type of discrimination is harassment against homosexuals rather than by homosexuals. The legal rights of homosexuals are being hotly debated, and employment discrimination based on an individual's sexual orientation is not currently protected by law.

Student-to-Student Sexual Harassment

Peer sexual harassment is the newest form of sexual harassment to be recognized by the courts. Evidence presented in a 1992 study conducted by the American Association of University Women (AAUW) documents that boys do not treat girls very well in our schools. Reports of unwelcome verbal and physical behavior of a sexual nature imposed by boys on girls in elementary, middle school and high schools are increasing. The AAUW report indicates that far too many school authorities do not view this as a serious occurrence and treat the behavior as an example of "boys being boys." Because of this unchecked behavior on the part of boys, many girls are reluctant to enroll in courses where they may be the only female.

Schools that do not stop peer sexual harassment may be liable to their students. During 1992 several school districts were held liable for the sexual harassment of students by other students. John Lewis, Susan Hastings and Anne Morgan report that an eighth grade student sued a San Francisco school district and her principal for unchecked peer harassment. The student alleged that boys repeatedly yelled "moo moo" and made vulgar references to her breasts and other body parts. The school district settled by paying the student $20,000. In another case, a Minnesota student charged her school district with sexual harassment for failing to remove graffiti that called her a "slut" and made other sexual comments about her. This school district settled the case for $15,000.

In April of 1993, the Chaska, Minnesota school district agreed to pay $40,000 to a former high school student to settle a complaint stemming from sexual harassment she suffered while in school. According to an article in *Education Week*, "this settlement is believed to be the largest nationwide to date in a student-to-student sexual harassment case." This case involved a complaint filed with the state human-rights department when the student discovered that her name was on a list circulated at the school that described her as sexually desirable and contained lewd and sexually graphic descriptions. School officials denied a request that the incident be used as a lesson on sexual harassment. Instead, they offered her counseling. The department ruled that the school district did not take timely and appropriate action on student-to-student sexual harassment.

Sexual harassment cases are not just occurring in our high schools. In a case that received a great deal of national media attention, a 7-year-old girl accused little boys of sexually harassing her on the school bus in Eden Prairie, Minnesota. In her complaint she stated that she was subjected to "multiple or severe acts" of harassment, including name-calling and unwelcome touching. According to Roger Murphey, public affairs officer for the Education Department, "the acts of sexual harassment were not confined to the school bus. It happened in the classroom, in the hallways, on the playground." In May of 1993 she won a historic battle when federal investigators concluded that her civil rights were violated by the school district. The case is the first in the United States involving student-to-student harassment among elementary age students. After a seven-month probe, the U.S. Department of Education's Office For Civil Rights accused the district of failing to respond properly to a "sexually hostile environment." Although the district did not admit any wrongdoing, it entered into a settlement with the federal government in which it agreed to be more vigilant in fighting sexual harassment.

A particularly interesting aspect of the school district's defense was their contention that they were obliged to treat some of the harassers more gently because they were emotionally disturbed students who qualify for special education under federal law. The Office for Civil Rights rejected this argument. In the letter of finding the Office for Civil Rights said, "The rights of students with disabilities may not operate as defense of behavior which singles out students, because of their sex, for adverse consequences."

One of the more important points in this case was made by Sue Sattel, sex equity specialist with the Minnesota Department of Education when she said, "The Office For Civil Rights is saying children don't even have to know what sex is to be sexually harassed. It's more about demeaning and degrading and making a hostile and intimidating environment."

Lewis, Hastings and Morgan report that a case is pending in Illinois where a girl's parents are seeking compensation for private school tuition and the costs of their child's counseling because third-grade elementary students pinched their daughter's chest, groin and buttocks on several occasions.

The number of cases alleging sexual harassment between peers in elementary and secondary schools is increasing. Although it is still too early to be able to define with certainty what courts will determine to be sexual harassment, it is clear that when a student is being harassed on the basis of his or her sex, it is sexual harassment.

Student-to-Teacher Sexual Harassment

As we conduct workshops and make presentations to students, teachers and administrators we are surprised by the number of teachers who asked us "is it possible for teachers to be sexually harassed by students?" As the teachers talked to us, it became clear that they knew that offensive behavior was taking place. What they wanted to know was, is this behavior sexual harassment? When we asked teachers to give us examples that they thought might be sexual harassment, we realized that we had to rethink the issue of power as a factor in sexual harassment.

Because of their age, education, maturity, experience, authority, and status it would seem that teachers have all of the power in the student-to-teacher relationship. However, teachers tell us that they have been embarrassed, degraded, undermined, and humiliated by students. Although not a scientific sample, we heard scores of stories of student to teacher sexual harassment. In each case the victim was a female teacher.

One teacher told of a group of male athletes that would crowd around her desk at the end of class and close in around her as she tried to walk out of the room. Another teacher, who was single and lived alone, told us that she often received obscene phone calls late at night. Other teachers told of having male students comment on their bodies, sex lives, and what the students could do to satisfy the teacher's need for sex.

In one discussion a male administrator said, "It is impossible for a teacher to be sexually harassed by a student...A competent teacher should be able to handle this type of behavior." He went on to say, "If a teacher had good classroom control, this type of behavior would not happen." His comments generated a heated debate between members of the group, and made it clear the student-to-teacher sexual harassment is not well understood. We asked the speaker what he would do if a female teacher was knocked to the ground and kicked in the hallway. He responded by saying that this was different. "This would be a case of assault and the students would be arrested." This exchange clearly demonstrates the tendency of men to blame the victim for her harassment. This administrator believed that it was some how the female teacher's fault that she was harassed. He believed that, either she did something to cause the harassment or she was not a good enough teacher to be able to prevent it.

Benson refers to sexual harassment of a victim who has formal power over the harasser as "counterpower" harassment. We are unaware of any studies that have examined this type of sexual harassment in public schools. However, Grauerholz conducted a study of this type of harassment by asking women college faculty members about behaviors directed toward them by students. He wanted to find out what behaviors occurred, whether the faculty members saw these behaviors as sexual harassment, and whether the professor had taken any actions to eliminate the behaviors. He found that the behaviors ranged from mild to severe, and there was a strong agreement that these behaviors constituted sexual harassment.

Sexist comments by male students toward female professors ranked as the most frequent form of sexual harassment. Approximately one in three faculty members indicated that they experienced this form of harassment. Other forms of harassment included: undue attention (18%), obscene phone calls (17%), verbal sexual comments (15 %), body language (12%), written comments (8%), sexual propositions (3%), physical advances (2%), sexual bribery (1%), and sexual assault (.5%). Almost two-thirds of the victims of this form of sexual harassment reported that they did nothing, and only three percent filed a formal complaint with the university.

Although at first glance "counterpower" sexual harassment seems to go against the generally accepted belief that sexual harassment is an abuse of power, Grauerholz argues that despite the women's formal authority in the university setting, the vulnerability of women professors to sexual harassment by male students reflected a cultural power difference between men and women. He believes that both a person's sex and status are factors that contribute to being a victim of sexual harassment.

Group Harassment

The most obscene and disgusting forms of sexual harassment involve groups of harassers. In 1993 the headlines were filled with stories of group harassment. In Los Angeles young men who called themselves the Posse competed for points for sexual conquests. Members of this group admitted to raping and molesting girls as young as 10 years old. In Glen Ridge, New Jersey 12 teenage boys gathered in a friend's basement to watch sexual acts performed on a mentally retarded 17 year old girl. The girl was sexually violated with a baseball bat, a stick, and a broom handle.

In *Peer Harassment: Hassles for Women on Campus*, O'Gorman Hughes and Sandler report that "men often do things in groups that they would not do alone....Whatever the reasons, when men are in a group they may say or do hostile things to women that they might not otherwise do as individuals....When men outnumber women...incidents of harassment are more likely to occur."

Several of the following examples of group harassment are adapted from Jean O'Gorman Hughes and Bernice Sandler's *Peer Harassment* .

√ "Scoping," describing and rating women's attractiveness on a scale of one to ten. This frequently occurs in libraries, study halls, cafeterias or other places where women pass by a group of men. This rating usually is accompanied by loud discussion of the woman's rating and her sexual attributes.

√ "Mooning," whereby men pull down their pants and show their buttocks aggressively. This is usually done by a group of men to one or more women.

√ "Sharking," whereby one male breaks away from a group of his friends and bites a woman on her breast.

√ "Spiking," whereby one or more males pull down the pants of a female.

√ "Flipping," whereby one or more males lift a girl's skirt up over her waist.

√ "Flashing," whereby one or more males expose their genitals to a single girl or group of girls.

Harassment by Non-Employees

It must be remembered that schools have an obligation to prevent sexual harassment in the school by *anyone*, including harassers who are not employed by the school district. Although we are not aware of any school-based court cases that have addressed this issue, we interpret the EEOC guidelines to mean that school districts are responsible for acts of sexual harassment by non-employees if the school administration knew or should have known of the conduct and failed to take immediate corrective action. The school is accountable for the actions of anyone who is in the school by invitation or with the permission of the school district. Consequently school districts should make sure that their notice against sexual harassment is prominently displayed.

Responsibility of School Employees to Supervise

Because students are compelled by state laws to attend school, they are not there by their own choice. Therefore, school children are protected by the Eighth Amendment of the U.S. Constitution, against state actions that constitute cruel and unusual punishment. States are increasingly holding school districts responsible for maintaining safe schools, in the belief that forcing children to attend crime-infested schools constitutes cruel and unusual punishment. California lead the nation in this area when it amended it's constitution to include the mandatory provision: "Right to Safe Schools." All students and staff of primary, elementary, middle/junior high and senior high schools have the inalienable right to attend campuses which are safe, secure and peaceful.

According to the National School Safety Center, "This amendment was passed because it was believed that school children are twice-victimized; (1) when they become actual victims of school-related crime, violence, disruption, or fear; and (2) when they are thereby denied their rights to a quality education in a tranquil learning environment."

Because courts commonly hold teachers and school districts liable for negligence, some courts are beginning to extend this accountability to protection from sexual harassment. If school administrators have previous knowledge of incidents of sexual harassment, they have an obligation to warn and protect potential victims. By the same token, if they know of previous violent or anti-social activities of a particular student, they need to take steps to prevent further violence.

Legal Protection Against Sex Discrimination

For the past twenty years legislators at the state and federal levels have been grappling with the issues surrounding sex discrimination. This struggle has resulted in laws being passed that set forth standards and procedures for ensuring nondiscrimination. The goal of all of these enactments is to ensure nondiscrimination and educational equity for both males and females. Sex discrimination in schools is prohibited by the following federal laws. The statutes, regulations and other legal sources mentioned below may be obtained from a law library, by contacting the agency responsible for enforcement, or a member of Congress.

Title VII of the Civil Rights Act of 1964 as amended by the Equal Employment Opportunity Act of 1972, the Pregnancy Discrimination Act of 1978 and the Civil Rights Act of 1991 prohibits employers employing more than 15 individuals from discriminating on the basis of race, color, religion, sex or national origin in all aspects of employment. The 1972 amendments permit employees and applicants to file suit in federal district court if they are not satisfied with the employers disposition of their complaints. This act covers all aspects of employment including pay, promotion, hiring, dismissal and working conditions. As amended in 1991, it allows sexual harassment plaintiffs to sue for monetary damages, allows recovery of compensatory damages only in cases of intentional discrimination and punitive damages only against non-public employers who act with malice or reckless indifference. The damages are currently capped depending on the number of employees.

In the fall of 1993 the U.S. Supreme Court is expected to hear arguments on a non-school sexual harassment case that could have significant implications for schools. The case of *Harris v. Forklift Systems* raises the question of whether employees alleging sexual harassment on the job must prove psychological injury in order to collect damages under Title VII. The Sixth Circuit Court of Appeals dismissed the case even after the plaintiff had shown that her boss subjected her to "a continuing pattern of sex-based derogatory conduct." The Court said she was unable to prove that the abuse affected her "psychological well-being." Two federal courts of appeal have agreed with the Sixth Circuit, but two others have held that plaintiffs need only prove the existence of a "hostile work environment" to be able to recover damages.

Women's Educational Equity Act of 1974 promotes educational equity for women through a program of discretionary grants and contracts. The act was reauthorized and substantially revised by the Education Amendments of 1978.

The **Carl D. Perkins Vocational Education Act of 1984** is a comprehensive effort to infuse sex equity into educational programs. This act requires positive action to end bias and stereotyping as well as to ensure nondiscrimination. It requires that each state hire at least one full-time staff person to coordinate and infuse sex equity throughout the vocational education system.

Executive Order 11246 as amended by Executive Order 11375 as amended by Executive Order 12086 prohibits employment discrimination in federal contracts. All federal contracts must contain a nondiscrimination clause in which the contractor agrees not to discriminate in any aspect of employment.

Title IX of the Education Amendments of 1972 prohibits discrimination on the basis of sex in educational programs or activities which receive federal financial assistance. Title IX covers both employees and students and virtually all activities of a school district. The prohibition covers discrimination in employment of teachers and other school personnel as well as discrimination in admissions, financial aid, and access to educational programs and activities. Title IX states: *"No person in the United States shall on the basis of sex be excluded from participating in, be denied the benefits of or be subjected to discrimination under any education program or activity receiving federal financial assistance."* In general, Title IX is enforced by the Department of Education. Under Title IX students may sue to collect monetary damages from the school or the school may lose federal funds.

State Laws. Every state has some form of gender discrimination law. As we mentioned earlier, the amount of attention that state legislatures have given to the issue of sexual harassment varies from state to state. To find out the applicable law in your state contact your state Civil Rights Commission located in the state capital.

When we make presentations on the legal rights of victims of sexual harassment and other forms of sex discrimination, we are frequently asked the following questions: Who can sue? How do you file a complaint? How long do I have to file a complaint? Who can make a complaint? How quickly must the investigation be completed? And, what are the punishments allowed? The following chart answers these questions.

Answers to Questions About
Federal Avenues for Redress

Entitlement	Who Can Sue	How Do I File	When Must I Act	Time For Investigation	Punishment Allowed
14th Amendment U.S. Constitution	Employees and students	Varies	Varies from state to state	Varies	Compensatory and punitive damages, and injunctive relief
Title VII	Employees and applicants	Complaints are called "charges" and can be in person, by letter or by EEOC form.	180 days to file charges with EEOC 90 days to sue in court.	120 days to complete investigation, "so far as practicable."	Courts may order behavior stopped and award relief, including back pay.
Title IX	Employees and students	By letter or complaint form obtained from Department of Education	180 days unless extended "for good cause"	Statute requires "prompt investigation."	Compensatory damages and injunctive relief.
Civil Rights Act of 1991	Employees and students	By letter or complaint form obtained from Department of Education	180 days unless extended "for good cause"	Statute requires "prompt investigation."	Compensatory damages and injunctive relief.

© 1993 Shoop and Hayhow, used by permission.

Proposed Federal Legislation

The growing national awareness of the way that girls are being shortchanged in our nations schools has resulted in the introduction of an omnibus legislative package. Anne Bryant, Executive Director of the American Association of University Women, calls this legislation "real progress toward providing America's girls with an educational environment that is equitable and free from bias." In April of 1993, The Gender Equity Education Act was introduced by Representatives Schroeder, Snowe, and Kildee. The package addresses the important areas of education reform related to gender equity including: teacher training; teen pregnancy and drop-out prevention; the establishment of an Office of Gender Equity in the Department of Education; funding for gender-fair teaching practices in math and science; the expansion of the Women's Educational Equity Act which promotes the use of gender equity programs and materials, and incentives to eliminate sexual harassment and abuse in schools. If approved, this act will amend the Elementary and Secondary Education Act of 1965.

Included in this package is H.B. 1795, The Sexual Harassment Free Schools Act. Representative Olympia Snowe introduced this bill for the purpose of authorizing a research and development front and an implementation grant for programs to address sexual harassment and violence. It would also expand the definition of an "effective schools program" to include an environment free from sexual harassment and abuse and would authorize funds under the Programs for the Improvement of Comprehensive School Health Education to be used for sexual harassment and assault programs.

Examples of Sexual Harassment

The following is a representative list of behaviors that a court might likely find to be sexual harassment.

√   A male teacher or student continually makes sexually explicit comments to a female student.

√   A male teacher propositions a female student.

√   A male teacher or student subjects female students to obscene pictures, unwanted touching and/or verbal sexual abuse.

√   A female student is depicted in sexually explicit cartoons or comments written on the boys' restroom walls.

√   A male teacher touches a female student repeatedly, makes suggestive comments, or asks her to have sex with him.

√   A group of male students stand in the halls and make sexual comments and proposition female students as they pass by.

√   Male teachers or students forcibly grab, hug, or kiss female students.

√   Male teachers or students flip up female students' dresses, pull down their pants, or grab their bodies.

√   Repeated and persistent requests for a date in the face of a clear indication of a lack of interest.

Examples Non-Sexual Harassment

√   A male teacher or student on one occasion pressed against a female student as they passed in the hallway.

√   A pin-up type photo is posted in the metal shop area, that is promptly removed at the order of the principal.

√   An isolated example of gender-related jokes or sexual teasing.

√   A single unwelcome request for a date.

Defenses Against Charges of Sexual Harassment

If a charge of sexual harassment is not able to be resolved within the school district and proceeds to the courts, there are some defenses that seem to be accepted and some that are rejected. According to the Utah Department of Human Resource Management, examples of defenses that may be allowed in sexual harassment cases include:

√   No harassment occurred.

√   Any advances were not unwelcome. They were solicited, incited or encouraged.

√   Harassment was not based upon sex, overtures were made to both sexes or conduct was equally offensive to both sexes.

√   Employer had legitimate non-discriminatory reasons for the conduct.

√   Harassment was not sufficiently severe or pervasive to alter the conditions of employment and create an abusive environment.

√   Employer had no knowledge of the harassment and there was a grievance avenue for claims.

√   Employer, with knowledge, took prompt and remedial action.

Examples of defenses that would probably not be considered in sexual harassment cases include:

√   The claimant's failure to verbalize disapproval of the sexually harassing behavior is not a protection for the behavior.

√   Whether or not the complainant participated voluntarily in the harassing behavior cannot be used as a defense for the accused.

√   Although a "sexually provocative" behavior, speech, dress and or demeanor may be admissible in a sexual harassment proceeding, it is not a defense for inappropriate behavior by the harasser.

Part Two
Pathways To Change

"As the human soul develops in us, we become able to grasp more fully our common needs and advantages; and with this growth has come the extension of eduction to the people as a whole."

Charlotte Perkins Gilman

Chapter Five

Policies and Procedures

When a student brings a charge of sexual harassment or reports an activity that appears to be a case of sexual harassment, the school should have a specific procedure to follow. Ideally, each school building should have a person trained and available so that students have someone to go to for advice without having to make a formal complaint. In this chapter we will present a description of the investigation process so that parents will be able to understand the appropriate steps that a school should follow. Parents should go to their child's school and ask to see the school's written policy and obtain a copy of the grievance procedure that will be used in cases of sexual harassment.

Conducting An Investigation

Each school building should have a person designated to monitor any complaints of sexual harassment. This person can be the principal, assistant principal, counselor or teacher. We recommend that at least one of the investigators of a sexual harassment complaint be of the same sex as the alleged victim. This person should ensure that all faculty and staff are trained in the identification and eradication of sexual harassment. This person should ensure that the sexual harassment policy is prominently displayed in the school, is printed in the student and teacher handbooks, and that all parents receive a copy of the policy. An orientation should be held for all students, parents, and teachers in which the policy and the consequences of sexual harassment is clearly explained. All students should also be instructed how to file a formal complaint of sexual harassment.

If a formal complaint is made, or if the sexual harassment compliance person believes that there is a probability that sexual harassment has occurred, he or she should talk with the person that was first contacted by the student, to get an overall picture of the situation.

A meeting should then be held with the student for the purpose of gathering as much information as possible, (i.e. What were the specific facts of the harassment? How long has the harassing behavior been going on? Were there any witnesses to the alleged harassment? What did the complainant do as a result of the harassment?) If the alleged harasser is a student, we strongly believe that the parents of both students should be brought into the process at this point. A false accusation of sexual harassment can seriously damage a student's reputation. We are also convinced that regardless of efforts to keep the investigation confidential, rumors will quickly begin to circulate. Parents have a right to know what is happening.

After a complaint is filed, the compliance person becomes the investigator. At this point, the investigator should decide who will be interviewed next, the harasser, other witnesses, or other victims. The investigator will have to decide this from initial information gathered from the student and/or teacher. If witnesses or other victims are not involved, or if the problem can be resolved between the harasser and the victim, the obvious choice is to talk to the person accused of the harassment. But if there are other victims, or if the student is afraid of the harasser, or if the harasser will become defensive, it may be best to interview the alleged harasser last.

At first, the initial list of individuals may be short. At the end of the interview, the investigator should ask if there are other people that may know something about this situation. The list of names should increase until the investigator is certain that he or she has enough information to make a determination. It is certainly better to do a thorough investigation and collect as much data as possible than to collect too little information.

The rights of the accused and the alleged victim are better served if the investigator asks open-ended questions. They should avoid yes/no questions such as "Did the harasser touch you? or Did the harasser make lewd remarks?" Questions should be phrased so the student can give more than a yes or no answer (i.e. "Please tell me about the situation" or "Give me some examples of the offensive behavior.") The investigator should remain neutral. He or she should keep calm and ensure that the atmosphere of the interview is as relaxed as possible. Webb suggests that the investigator should; (1) avoid expressing opinions, (2) not take sides, (3) develop the list of questions before the interview process starts, and (4) remember to ask the same questions of all parties interviewed.

The investigation should begin with an introduction by the investigator at which time the investigator should make it clear that he or she will be impartial and fair to all individuals. All parties involved must understand that the only purpose of the investigation is to gather data and resolve the problem. It is imperative that all information must be a true and accurate reporting of things they heard or saw. Although confidentiality must be protected as much as possible, it is impossible to guarantee that names and situations may not be reported. A final report should be made with recommendations to the school board. All people who are questioned must be told that they are free to ask any questions. The involved parents should be informed at the conclusion of the investigation, regardless of the outcome.

To ensure that accurate and complete information is gathered the investigator might ask the following questions:

1. Describe the offensive behavior.
2. Where did it take place?
3. When did it take place?
4. How many times did it occur?
5. Describe your feelings at the time the harassment occurred.
6. What was your response at the time the harassment occurred?
7. Did you tell anyone about the incident after it occurred?
8. Who did you tell, when, and what did you tell that person?

9. What was that person's response?

10. Describe any incidents of retaliation.

11. Show me any documentation that you have of the offensive behavior. (Journals, pictures, cartoons, jokes, etc.)

12. Who witnessed the incident?

Script of Questions to Ask Witnesses:

1. One of your students or fellow students has complained about some behaviors of (name alleged harasser.) Tell me what you know about the situation. (If the person describes harassment, the same questions may be asked as were asked of the complainant. If the person doesn't know anything, the next two questions might be asked.)

2. Have you ever had a problem with either person?

3. Do you know anybody who can clarify the situation?

Script of Questions to Ask Alleged Harasser:

1. One of your students or fellow students (name student) has complained about some of your behaviors at school. Can you tell me more about the situation?

2. (Describe some of the behaviors reported by the named student.) Can you tell me anything that will clarify the situation?

3. Have you ever had a problem with (name of student)?

The investigator should end all interviews by strongly stating that this situation is not to be discussed in order to protect the rights and privacy of the people involved. All parties should be told that if they are asked about the situation they are to say they have been asked not to discuss it. The witnesses should be told approximately when the investigation will be completed. It is very important that the investigator make it clear that no retaliation will be tolerated.

During the interview, detailed notes should be taken. Key phrases should be written down so that details can be filled in after the interview. Webb suggests that because it is not necessary that every word be written exactly, it is not necessary that a tape recorder be used. However, she believes that it is very important that accurate notes are kept and that details be immediately written after the interview before doing any further investigation.

After the investigation is complete, the investigator should look for common threads in the interview notes when analyzing the data. The EEOC guidelines and the local school policy should be used as the criterion for determining if sexual harassment has taken place. For example, was the behavior unwelcome, not asked for, not returned? Was it deliberate and/or repeated sexual or sex-based behavior?

Confronting Harassers

Parents must let their daughters know that they understand that confronting a student or teacher harasser is not an easy thing to do. However, we must let our daughters know that they have a right to be free from harassment and have a right to see that sexual harassment is stopped. It is important to empower female students with the knowledge that they have the right to be free from harassment and the power to see that they are not bothered. Students who experience sexual harassment want the harassment stopped. They don't want to be punished for complaining and they want to go to school in an atmosphere free of sexual harassment. When confronted with sexual behavior, students should be told to assess the situation and determine whether the behavior is unwanted. If it is, then the student should take action to stop it.

As we said earlier, it is common for a victim of sexual harassment to try to ignore the offensive behavior. In a recent study that we conducted, we found that the most frequent response to sexual harassment was to "discuss it with a friend." Only 19% told the principal and only 18% told their parents.

According to Sandroff, approximately one-third of the harassers who were told to stop, did so. If the sexual harassment is ignored, the harasser can argue that he thought the activity was welcomed by the victim. Victims of sexual harassment must make it clear to the harasser that the behavior is inappropriate and that it must stop. Because sexual harassment is a matter of perception, the victim's perception of the behavior must be made visible if she wants to avoid further harassment. The harasser must be put on notice that the line has been crossed, the behavior is offensive, and that it will not be tolerated.

Debbie Edwards suggests that students who are victims of sexual harassment take the following steps when confronting the harasser.

• **Be assertive**. Be honest and direct. Say you find the behavior offensive. Don't apologize ("I'm sorry, but I didn't like..."). You are being harassed, not the other way around. Don't hint or be evasive ("I'm busy tonight or I have other plans."), say clearly that you aren't interested. Some men still claim that women mean yes when they don't specifically say no. So say no clearly ("The answer is no. Don't ask again." Or, "I've told you before that I'm not interested in that kind of relationship. Stop asking me."). Body language is important when confronting a harasser. Your tone of voice should be even and firm, make eye contact, be aware of your posture (don't hunch or fold your arms in front of you), and be as confident as possible. If you are nervous about confronting your harasser, then rehearse what you will say with a friend.

• **Write the harasser a letter**. While some people may be able to be assertive, others may not feel comfortable in speaking directly to a harasser. Another excellent way to confront a harasser is to write a letter. In the letter, describe the behavior that is offensive and why you object to it. Be very direct. If you don't, then the letter will be ineffective and you won't accomplish what you want to do, ending the offensive behavior. Get a second opinion from a person you trust to see if the letter is clear. If you feel the harassment will escalate, let the harasser know what action you will take to get it to stop. You may want to attach a copy of your school's sexual harassment policy to the letter. Keep a copy of the letter for future records as it will serve as valuable evidence later if needed. Above all, do what you say you will do in the letter. Don't make idle threats (see appendix B for sample letter).

The concept of writing a letter was originated by Mary Rowe and further developed by Bernice Sandler. Sandler reminds us that "the letter should be polite, low key and detailed, and consist of...a factual account,...describe how the writer feels about the events,...and include what the writer wants to happen next." Sandler suggests that the letter be delivered in person or by registered or certified mail. She cautions that copies not be sent to anyone else and that the writer should keep a copy.

• **Document the incidents**. Note the date, time, and place that the harassment occurred. Include the names of everyone involved, particularly if you have witnesses that can verify what happened. It is important to describe the event in as much detail as you can. Your documentation should be as contemporaneous with the event as possible. The EEOC and many courts have strongly supported the value of a contemporaneous complaint or protest. Describe the harassers words and behavior. Write down what you said, what you did, and how you felt (Is the harassment affecting your school performance or health?). When you make a formal complaint, keep a copy for your records. Keep your journal in a safe place and keep an additional copy at home.

• **Collect evidence**. If you are going to school in a hostile learning environment, do whatever you can to collect the evidence. If there are cartoons, jokes, etc. posted on the bulletin board, anything that makes you feel uncomfortable, confiscate them. William Petrocelli and Barbara Repa recommend that if you can't take the offensive items, at least make a copy or take a photograph of the material. If the offensive material is in the boy's restroom have a friend copy the exact language for you. If you are unable or unwilling to take the offensive material, you should describe the material in as much detail as possible and put a copy in your journal.

• **Check with other students**. You should assume there is no such thing as a first time sexual harasser. Ask your friends if something similar has happened to them. A complaint backed up by others makes retaliation less likely and gives support to your complaint.

• **Keep copies of your grades and graded work**. If the harasser is a teacher, you should be able to document any adverse grade or treatment that has occurred as a result of your refusal.

• **File a formal complaint**. If the sexual harassment continues you should make a formal complaint. Some students do not make formal complaints because they do not understand that they have a right to be free from sexual harassment at school. Students want to fit in with their friends and the drug of peer acceptance is addictive. However, sexual harassment and retaliation is illegal.

If you are being sexually harassed by a teacher or a fellow student you have the right to make a formal complaint. Although it is sometimes hard to take this action, sexual harassment will likely get worse if unreported. Sandler offers a word of caution. She warns that the student should stop and think before she takes any action. Because any action you take may provoke a reaction, be sure of what you are going to say and what you want to happen.

What Parents Can Do

Some people believe that the only way to stop sexual harassment is through legislative action and law suits. However, we believe that there are at least five distinct and important steps that parents must take in order to eradicate sexual harassment in schools.

First, everyone must recognize that a serious problem exists. It is hard for many parents to acknowledge that school is not the place it once was. It is comforting to believe that when our children leave our care and enter school they will be safe and all of their experiences will be positive. However, this is not reality. We have to recognize that sexual harassment exists before we can stop it.

Second, parents, teachers, and students need to understand and analyze the causes of sexual harassment before we can take productive action. The third step involves allowing ourselves to feel the outrage that is necessary in order for us to do more than wish our schools were free of sexual harassment. Fourth, we must talk to our children, their teachers, and their administrators and explain the serious consequences of sexual harassment. We must help them see the connection between sexual stereotyping, sexism, and sexual harassment. And finally, we must insist that our school district develop a comprehensive policy prohibiting all forms of sexual harassment, train all staff and students, and then monitor behavior to ensure that sexual harassment is not taking place in our schools.

What Students Can Do

Most victims of sexual harassment use informal remedies to resolve sexual harassment. If a student believes that the person that is harassing her does not know that the behavior is offensive, simply asking or telling him to stop often makes things better. Threatening to tell a teacher, a counselor, or your parent is also an effective action. If the offensive behavior continues you may wish to file an official grievance through your school's grievance procedure. If you are still being bothered you can file a discrimination complaint or contact an attorney and file a lawsuit.

Every student should be certain that their school has a policy prohibiting sexual harassment, and that every teacher and student is aware of the policy. If a student is harassed, he or she must be certain to let the harasser know that the advances are not welcome.

If you even suspect that something is not right or that you are being sexually harassed, you should immediately tell your parents about the offensive behavior. It is very helpful if you write down the date, times, and your best memory of what was said or done to you during the harassment. If the harassment persists, inform a trusted teacher, counselor, or administrator. Report any efforts at retaliation, reduction of grade, loss of privilege, or threats by the harasser or his friends.

If you believe that your school is not adequately responding to your complaints, you may wish to initiate a formal grievance action. If you are not satisfied with the outcome of the school district's investigation, you may contact your state Office for Civil Rights, the U.S. Department of Education Office of Civil Rights or obtain the services of an attorney.

What You Should Not Do

O'Gorman Hughes and Sandler advise that there are three things that victims of sexual harassment should avoid at all costs:

√ **Don't blame yourself.** Sexual harassment is not something that a woman brings on herself, it is action that the harasser decides to take. It is not your fault. Blaming yourself only turns your anger inward and can lead to depression. You need to turn your anger outward, against the appropriate person, the harasser.

√ **Don't delay.** If you delay action when someone harasses you, it is likely to continue. Also, if you intend to file charges against someone and put off doing so for a long time, you may find out that you have missed the time limit for doing so.

√ **Don't keep it to yourself.** By being quiet about sexual harassment, you enable it to continue. Chances are extremely good that you are not the only victim. Speaking up can protect other people from also becoming victims. Additionally, not telling anyone encourages feelings of helplessness and can also lead to blaming yourself for the incident.

Chapter Six

Persuading Your School and State

The Problem

Schools, like most institutions, are traditional, stable, and slow to change. However, society is very fluid and change is occurring constantly. Consequently, many school board members and state legislators do not recognize that the rules for appropriate behavior have changed. Because they often do not understand the seriousness of sexual harassment, they have done little to combat it.

Many teachers and administrators do not know what sexual harassment is, and do not recognize their responsibility to stop it. An example is the Eden Prairie case that we discussed earlier, that involved a seven year old girl who was subjected to repeated sexual harassment while riding on the school bus. The principal said the behavior could not be sexual harassment because the offending boys were too young to understand what they were doing. The Department of Education's Office of Civil Rights reminded the principal and the school district that intent is not the critical issue in sexual harassment cases. Courts look at the impact of the actions on the victims. In most school districts there are no policies that even address the issue of student-to-student sexual harassment.

Because we live in a democracy, school boards and state legislatures are held accountable and responsible to us. They are not allowed to operate irresponsibly and arbitrarily. We have the opportunity to elect them and to freely express our opinions. Simply having the freedom to say what we think is not a guarantee of a democratic system. We must also have the reasonable expectation of continually keeping our elected representatives responsive to us. Democracy, like any other form of government, is a system of power. In a democracy, school boards and state legislatures are created to act as mediators between the various conflicting demands. They are charged with attempting to formulate policies and statutes that benefit the public. Most decisions are compromises that seldom satisfy all interested parties. The goal of a democratic government is to work for a consensus that allows every group to have a say.

Much of the following information about lobbying is adapted from a monograph written by Robert Shoop and Lynn Hellebust. Lobbying is a method of working within the political structure to bring about desired change. For our purposes, lobbying is essentially a system of communication aimed at influencing the decision-making process. It is an effort to affect the perceptions of school board members and members of state legislatures about sexual harassment and to influence their decisions relative to sexual harassment.

In order to ensure that sexual harassment is eradicated from our schools, we must build a climate of opinion favorable to equity and then directly affect legislation and policy development. Lobbying is essential to a democracy in order to provide people with effective channels to pressure government to achieve our goals. Our system of government is based on the assumption that struggle between contending groups produces the best public policy. People who want to bring about change must understand that public policy results from bargaining, negotiation, and compromise between various groups, each attempting to maximize its power and influence.

The lobbying process may be either positive-seeking legislation and policies affirming equal treatment, or negative-trying to prevent government from acting in a manner that encourages harassment or protects harassers. In order to be effective, lobbying efforts must (1) focus on a specific policy area, (2) communicate accurate and persuasive information, and (3) include sophisticated lobbying skills.

One of the basic goals of anti-sexual harassment legislation is to restructure our schools so that they encourage and enhance equal opportunity and discourage all forms of discrimination and harassment. If our efforts succeed, our schools will be modified in concrete and observable ways. The most obvious modification would be the requirement that each school system have a comprehensive sexual harassment policy and that every educator and every student be trained to recognize and eradicate all forms of sexual harassment.

As a general rule, mobilization to organize and have a school district policy approved can happen rather rapidly. Whereas, mobilization and organization to enact state legislation takes a long time. Whether at the local level or the state level, the process usually follows a three stage progression (1) the beginning stage, (2) the stage of enthusiastic involvement, and (3) the period of institutionalization of what began as an emerging value into the main stream of the core culture.

For most of us, the whole concept of lobbying is new, and perhaps conjures up negative images of dishonesty and corruption.

However, it must be remembered that the lobbying process, and in turn the legislative process, allows the issue of sexual harassment in the schools to be lifted from the hands of parents and other people without formal power and forces the people with the formal power, school board members and legislators, to deal with and act on this important issue.

Sexual harassment cannot be eliminated from our schools unless we give careful attention to the political realities of procedural tactics and strategies. People who want to change school policy or state legislation must be aware of factors such as timing, public opinion, degrees of controversy, related power of the various school board members and legislators, as well as the step-by-step procedure involved in getting a specific policy changed or a specific piece of legislation passed into law.

Although there are a number of negative connotations associated with the term "lobbying," it is essentially a neutral term that means attempting to influence the outcome of a legislative decision.

There are basically four things you need to know in order to successfully influence a school board or a state legislature. First, you must have a thorough knowledge of sexual harassment and its legislative history. Secondly, you have to understand the organization and structure of the school board and of the legislature, that is, how they work. Thirdly, you have to know something about the more influential board members and legislators, what makes them tick. Finally, you must have some idea of how to successfully put all the parts together.

Thoroughly Understand Sexual Harassment

It may seem obvious, but make sure that your spokespersons are as knowledgeable as possible about sexual harassment. It is important to remember that it often takes a different type of leader to mobilize a lobbying effort than it might have taken to start the movement. Often new types of leaders appear as a movement progresses, leadership geared more to the specific efforts of eradicating sexual harassment (i.e. lobbying) rather than the general ideals and goals of gender equity. Issues of stability, growth, and tactics are of crucial importance. However, the new leader must have a solid philosophical and historical understanding of the problems associated with sexual harassment if he or she is going to be able to lead a successful lobbying effort. This leader must not only understand the legal aspects of eradicating sexual harassment, but also the arguments for not acting to eradicate sexual harassment from our schools.

It is also important to know the legislative history of sexual harassment in your state and sexual harassment policies in your school district. Has the issue of sexual harassment in general, or in the schools, been studied or debated in previous years? What happened? What school board members or legislators supported or opposed it? Are they still around? What individuals and organized interests were involved? Also, are there any board policies or legislation currently under consideration? In what form? Have policies or bills been introduced? How many and by whom? Which bills represent serious efforts? Which bills do you support?

It is important to do this portion of your homework well, because the first time you approach a school board member or legislator with the thought of influencing (rather than just gathering information) you want to be able to hold your own in a discussion of the issue.

After you are confident that you are an expert on sexual harassment, it is imperative for you to have more than a general idea of how your local school board and state legislature functions. While school boards and legislatures vary in the particulars, there are, nevertheless, common patterns.

How Local School Boards Work

Most people don't know exactly what their school board actually does. And few people know the names of their school board members. The nations' slightly more than 15,000 local school boards were created to give local citizens immediate access to the policy-making process.

Local school boards are made up of lay citizens who are elected to provide policy-level guidance for education. Although local school boards are created by state legislatures, courts tend to uphold the majority of decisions made by local school boards. Local boards of education are very important in implementing policy at the local level.

The development of policies is one of the most important responsibilities of school boards. The establishment of policy is one way in which people exert control, influence, or power over each other. Policy development at the school district level is influenced by state and federal laws, court decisions, and the desires of the local citizens. According to Patricia First, policies are passed by boards of education in order to inform the community about the school board's philosophy, intents, and goals. They are supposed to eliminate school district confusion in all areas and at all levels of school district management.

The policy process is political, and lobbying and other forms of overt political action are ways that citizens can influence policy outcomes. The policy cycle is a process that usually starts with someone bringing an issue to the attention of a school board member. Assuming that the school board member recognizes the seriousness of the issue, a study group is often formed. This group develops policy recommendations, and suggests a plan for implementation. After a policy is developed, a specific implementation procedure is usually written.

How State Legislatures Work

Most state legislatures meet every year, although some still meet every other year. While the average state legislature is still a "citizen's" legislature, in that it does not meet full time, study committees often hold extensive hearings between legislative sessions. You will first need to know whether your legislature meets every year and if it utilizes interim study committees. With the exception of Nebraska, all state legislatures are bicameral, that is, they consist of two houses called the senate and the house of representatives.

Legislative Organization

Almost all legislatures begin in January. Most have completed their session by May or June. Some go on into summer and less than half a dozen meet year around. The situation is complicated a bit by the fact that some states also hold special sessions fairly frequently. So, first of all ,you need to find out when, and for how long your legislature meets.

You also need to be aware of how many legislators there are in your legislature, and which party holds control in each house. In addition to knowing which political party controls each house you should also be aware of any significant groups or coalitions of legislators that may exist in either house. Legislators, of course, are elected by the people of the district they represent. The most common term of office is four years for the senate and two years for the house of representatives.

Next, you need to know who your legislative leaders are. In all states the speaker is the leader in the house of representatives. In the senate the top leadership position is either the president or president pro tem. In those states where the lieutenant governor presides over the senate, the majority party elects a president pro tem who normally is the real power in the state's senate.

Legislative bodies do most of their work through their committees. The number of committees in the senate or house may run from less than 10 to more than 30. As you will see, committees have a life and death hold on bills assigned to them. And chairpersons of the more important committees are normally powerful members of the legislative leadership.

Legislative Process

The process by which a bill becomes a law has many points of access. In order for you to succeed in getting sexual harassment free schools legislation passed, you must succeed at every step along the way. However, you must remember that your opponents can kill your bill if they succeed at any one point. This is an important point to remember because whether you are trying to pass or kill a bill will make a big difference in the strategy you will employ.

Every member of the legislature has the power to introduce a bill. In most legislatures members can prefile bills prior to the convening of the legislature and continue filing bills until a cutoff time provided in the legislature's rules. A bill's "first reading" comes when a clerk announces the title and number to the full house. In choosing a sponsor for the legislation you want to have introduced, you must proceed with caution. Be careful to choose a sponsor who is respected and who it regarded as having some expertise in the subject matter.

We have seen enthusiastic groups who had developed a bill that they wanted to have passed flounder at this point. In one case we attended a meeting where the chairperson asked if anyone knew a member of the state house of representatives. When a member of the audience said he did, that representative was targeted to serve as a sponsor of the bill. As it turns out, that representative was serving in his first term, had no power, and did not serve on the appropriate committees. Needless to say, the bill did not become a law.

A senior member of the committee the bill will likely be assigned to is a good choice. Make sure your sponsor will work for the passage of the bill. And be sure to give careful consideration as to which house your bill should be introduced in, because there may be less resistance in one than in the other.

After introduction, a bill is usually referred to one of the standing committees for consideration. In some states all bills introduced are automatically referred to a committee by the speaker on the house and normally by the president or a special committee in the senate. In other states, a bill sometimes will not be referred. In many cases, the committee a bill will be referred to is clear cut, in others it is not. In these situations, getting a bill assigned to the most favorable committee becomes very important.

Normally, the most important step in the process is committee consideration of a bill. In most states, every bill referred to a committee is considered or "heard," in some fashion, by the full committee or a subcommittee. Most major bills have a hearing which determines a bill's fate.

It is imperative that you learn all you can about the relative power of committee chairpersons in your state and that you learn as much as possible about all members of the committee to which your bill is assigned. Generally speaking, appropriations and tax committees are composed of more experienced and able legislators than many of the other committees. Be aware of the general nature of the committee you're dealing with.

What kind of notice will be given when, and if, a hearing is to be held on your bill will depend on the state. In this regard you should work closely with, and follow the advice of, the legislator sponsoring your bill. Whether a hearing is held or not, a committee has a number of options open to it. For one thing, it can simply sit on a bill. It can report the bill out of the committee with a favorable recommendation, or with a negative recommendation. Just what these reports are called varies from state to state, and this terminology is part of the local language you will need to learn.

At this stage, if permitted, a bill is debated by the whole house and floor amendments are offered. In most cases, if a committee reports a bill out favorably, the bill will be scheduled for consideration by the whole house. This means the bill usually will be included on a printed calendar which indicates when it likely will come up for consideration. In most states bills may be amended at this point. In other states amendment would be difficult. It is at this point, sometimes called "second reading," that legislative rules and customs vary a good deal from state to state, another reason why you need to learn how your particular legislature operates in some detail, if you are to be successful in your lobbing efforts. You need to know what the formal rules provide, and when they are followed, and when they are not.

Following floor consideration, a bill is put to a final vote, sometimes called "third reading." In some states a majority of the total membership of the house is required to pass a measure. In others only a majority of those voting is necessary. Rules usually provide for a way to reconsider, but whether that is actually done very often will depend on the custom and traditions of your state. If defeated in one house, a bill is usually dead for that session.

If a bill passes the first house it goes to the second house where it must go through the same process all over again, except in Nebraska, which has only one house. If the bill survives the second house without an amendment, it goes on to the governor. If the second house amends the bill, the first house may go along with the change, in which case the bill then goes to the governor. If the two chambers disagree, a conference committee is formed to resolve the differences between them.

The Governor

One way or another, a bill surviving the legislative gauntlet goes to the governor for consideration, except in North Carolina. (In North Carolina, the governor has neither the power to approve or disapprove bills.) A governor has several options. He or she may sign the bill, permit it to become law without his or her signature, or veto the bill.

When a governor vetoes a bill he or she returns it along with a veto message to the legislature. However, a bill can still become law if both houses have enough votes (usually two-thirds is required) to "override" the veto. One other possibility exists in a number of states. In these states if the legislature adjourns before the time a governor has to sign a bill runs out, thereby preventing the return of the bill along with the veto message, the bill dies if the governor chooses not to sign it.

What You Need To Know

Whether it is a crucial committee chairperson, someone you would like to sponsor a bill or your local legislator, there is probably a good deal of public information available about the person that will help you understand "where he or she is coming from."

First, of course, you want to make sure you have the legislator's name correct, then both address and telephone number at home and in the state capitol, along with the individual's age, marital status (children, if any), and religion. Educational background is helpful, as is some notion of the organizations or associations to which the legislator belongs.

An idea of the legislator's political history is a necessity. When was he or she first elected to the legislature? What public or party offices has he or she held previously? Who was his or her opponent in the last election and what was the vote? To what committees is he or she assigned? And, does he or she hold any leadership positions?

Then, of course, you need to be aware of the legislator's occupation and other financial interests and business dealings. Most certainly you should know who has been the major financial contributors to the legislator's campaigns, and, in particular, what interest groups have supported him or her. Such information tells you with what sorts of people and organizations a legislator is comfortable. Also, a socioeconomic description of the legislator's district is useful. These kinds of information are usually available from public sources.

It also becomes imperative to know what kind of person the legislator is. Is he or she liberal or conservative? And does he or she deviate from or tend to vote the way his or her district thinks? Is he or she honest or dishonest, informed or uninformed? Is he or she bright or a little slow, conscientious or superficial? How strong is the influence of his or her political party on him or her? Is he or she a regular or a maverick? In what subjects does he or she specialize and is he or she respected and looked to for advice in those areas or is he or she avoided?

In many ways legislators are like the rest of us. Sometimes the reason why they do a particular thing is simple and straight forward, and sometimes it is involved and complex. Often their behavior is not motivated by a single reason or purpose, but by a mixture. Some respond to their own internal objectives, others to encouragement, and others to threats. In other ways they are different. After all, they have successfully run for office and are concerned with re-election. They tend to be more knowledgeable about public affairs and they are inclined to greater feelings of self-importance than most people.

There are a number of factors that influence a legislator's vote. If you are going to try to have an impact on a piece of legislation, you need to know enough about the legislators you will be dealing with to know which approaches to use and which to avoid.

Generally speaking, the more controversial and visible an issue, the harder it will be for a legislator to decide how to vote. The less controversial and visible the issue, the easier it is for a legislator to make a decision because the likelihood of political consequences is also less. The less controversial and visible the issue, the more likely a decision will be motivated by self-interest or the interests of a small group rather that the legislator's constituency as a whole.

In addition, on many, if not most issues, a legislator has no prior position, and he or she is open to suggestion. On such issues someone with access to a legislator can contribute significantly to the decision the legislator will make. That's why lobbyists and others spend time and money getting to know legislators, so that they will have access when the time comes for them to talk in earnest about an issue.

Often the most important factors in determining how a legislator will vote is the way his or her constituents will view the vote and the extent to which they would be motivated to retaliate in the next election if the vote goes contrary to their wishes. This is particularly true regarding issues of interest to the more powerful among a legislator's constituents. Philosophically, there is not likely to be much public opposition to a bill which is aimed at eliminating sexual harassment from schools. The problems are likely to revolve around the question of how much money this effort is going to cost the taxpayers.

Also, keep in mind that the justification and quality of the arguments put forth for a bill or an idea can be quite important. Therefore, when you're pushing an issue, your persuasive ability can be pivotal. Think out your arguments ahead of time. Often your legislator may be looking for a reason to support your position. Give him or her solid, rational reasons to do so.

You must also be able to deal with questions of whether the bill you're in favor of, or opposed to, would actually do what you say it will. In other words, will it work? And always know what the cost of your proposal would be. And be aware of whether the measure could be declared unconstitutional if passed.

Several of these next points cause us some discomfort, because we see significant problems with Political Action Committees. We would like to believe that legislators are all motivated by what is best for the largest number of people. However, in reality, there are other factors that play an important part in legislative decision making. For example, personal factors can become important to a legislator, especially when an issue is not very visible. Will the proposed bill financially help a legislator's business or profession? Are a legislator's personal beliefs or governmental philosophy a factor? And, on occasion, a legislator may trade votes with another legislator, that is, vote one way on an issue of importance to another legislator in return for that legislators vote on a different matter. The position taken by a legislator's party or leadership may also be a factor in how a legislator votes.

These are some of the things that can and do influence the way a legislator votes. You need to analyze your situation and use those factors that help your position and downplay those that work against you.

How to Put It All Together

Having acquired a working knowledge of the issues surrounding sexual harassment, your local school board, and your legislature, you must now give some thought to how to put it all together in order to successfully influence the outcome of a policy or legislative decision. You, either individually or through some organization, need a strategy. It may be simple or complex, but you need some idea of where you're headed and how you're going to get there.

You need to create a situation that will make it to a school board member's or legislator's advantage to vote in your favor. Base your strategy on an awareness of how a majority of the school board or legislature will tend to vote on your issue under varying circumstances.

Remember, above all most school board members and most state legislators want to be re-elected. So your strategy must not threaten his or her re-election. In fact, in a subtle manner, you must convince each school board member or each legislator that voting your way is the shortest path to re-election. You must also be aware that there are always some board members and legislators looking ahead to running for a higher office, as well as those considering retirement.

One strategy is to develop and emphasize widespread public support for eradicating sexual harassment. To do this you must stress the mobilization of support for this position and the involvement of public officials or prominent civic leaders. Your strategy should also stress the un-workability, high cost and unconstitutionality of a school environment which permits sexual harassment.

Much of lobbying is a personal sort of undertaking hinging on your personality, your contacts, and that part of society you represent. Depending on the circumstances, you may want to play the issue in a public forum. Because sexual harassment affects all students, the public approach suggests itself.

There are some general warnings. First of all, start early. If your state uses an interim study period between legislative sessions, use that period to begin your effort. Then be prepared to compromise. Most proposals must ultimately be adapted somewhat during the legislative give-and-take. So be prepared for it and know which parts of your proposal you can give on and which you can't. Then build coalitions. If at all possible, reach out to individuals, businesses, and groups which would be able to support you and increase public involvement. Remember that a proposal rarely succeeds the first time around. Most major pieces of legislation, if they are ultimately passed, take several years. Be committed to the long haul. Don't allow yourself to become discouraged at initial failures.

Lobbying Techniques

When you get to the point of actually trying to influence the behavior of school board members or legislators, you are, by most definitions, lobbying. And the lobbying techniques you will employ depend not only on your expertise and personality, but also on the character and personality of the school board member or legislator you are dealing with. The better you know them, the better you can adjust the way in which you communicate with them.

Lobbying techniques can be divided into two general approaches, direct and indirect. In the direct approach you attempt to work with key legislators and committees. The indirect approach involves generating support among a particular constituency, the public at large, or the mass media. Rarely will you utilize one approach to the exclusion of the other. Rather, it is a matter of emphasis.

What kinds of things can you do on a direct personal level? First, prepare research and background material. This does not mean that you have to create the support material. The various appendixes in this book provide listings of a wide range of groups that have generated volumes of documentation about sexual harassment. There is no need to attempt to reinvent the wheel. It is our experience that most of these organizations are more than willing to assist anyone trying to eradicate sexual harassment.

Next, make your argument by presenting your facts directly to your school board member or legislator. It is helpful at this point if you have examples of policies and state legislation upon which your school board policy or state legislation can be modeled (see Appendix B). We have provided sample policies and state legislation in the appendixes. Arrange to have a bill introduced by the best sponsor. Try to have the bill referred to the most favorable committee and attempt to persuade the committee to act favorably. Testify at hearings and arrange for others to testify. Do what you can to head off potential opposition.

Whether you are visiting legislators in their districts between sessions, in their offices, or on their way to the floor for a vote will govern what and how much can be discussed. Whatever the occasion, always be pleasant and well prepared. Identify the bill by number and subject, especially when you are meeting a legislator for the first time. Describe the impact of the proposed bill. Be clear about what you want your legislator to do. Politely request an answer, but don't back your legislator into a corner if he or she is reluctant to make a commitment. On your first visit make sure you leave the legislator a short position statement. And always thank him or her.

In developing a position statement designed to be left with or provided to legislators, be brief. Remember that they are extremely busy with many different agendas and volumes of reading material. Make it one page if at all possible. If you need more space, cover your material with a one or two page summary. Use a clear, outline format and set each point out separately. State the problem first and follow with the legislative remedy you are seeking with the supporting reasons developed point by point. Be honest about advantages as well as the disadvantages of the course of action you are seeking. Let the legislator know who will support and who will oppose your proposal and why. Remember to address cost and practical problems such as implementation, as well as constitutional and legal problems.

Because lobbying is in large part an educational process, you will spend much of your time answering questions and providing background information on your issue. The character of this aspect of your effort will depend, in part, on how large a research and reference staff the legislator has. Bill drafting at the state level is almost always a highly specialized and closely controlled function of a bill drafting office under the direction of the legislature. So you should expect that whatever draft you offer as a vehicle for your idea will be reworded before it is introduced.

Your appearance before the committee is your chance to present your argument for your legislation. Be as brief as you can. Prepare thoroughly. Spend some time talking to opponents of the proposal, legislators, other lobbyists, people who you might expect may testify against your position. This will enable you to view the issue from a variety of perspectives. It will also help you to anticipate questions and prepare answers. Keep your testimony brief and to the point. Use examples whenever possible that are reflective of interests of the legislators on the committee. For example, it would be helpful if you know of one exemplary model sexual harassment policy from each legislator's district. Having some of these school districts represented by their local community members is also a good tactic.

Organize the number and order of other supportive testimony. The last person who testifies should conclude with a concise summary of the most important points presented. Have copies of all key points to leave for the committee to review.

Gear some of your arguments to persuade committee members who are sitting on the fence, and include some press worthy quotes. Try to make sure that those committee members committed to your cause are present, if not for the hearing, then certainly for the vote.

Remember that nothing will happen to your bill unless someone takes an interest in it, so monitor it carefully. Know where it is at all times and let your legislative supporters in both houses know the bill's status. And always keep track of who stands where on the bill, right up to the governor. Many an elated and battle scarred veteran of legislative battles has relaxed too soon only to witness the governor's veto wipe out months of effort.

A Grassroots Approach

If you pursue the indirect, or grassroots approach, you will still need to utilize a number of the direct means of accessing legislators previously mentioned. However, because of limited access to some key legislators and because many legislators do not understand the issue of sexual harassment, you may need to impress them with the popularity of your cause.

Normally, the most effective indirect method of influencing the legislator or school board member is to generate constituent action. This can be done on a limited scale by urging key constituents or friends of the legislator to contact him or her about the sexual harassment legislation. If you can muster significant district-wide strength, mobilize a general write-in campaign directed at the legislators from those districts. The development of alliances among interest groups can be very useful in demonstrating grassroots support.

Grassroots lobbying efforts are a legitimate function of anyone who wants anti-sexual harassment legislation passed. Such efforts normally involve public relations campaigns to persuade people to contact their legislators in support of your cause. If you choose this route, you will need to become proficient in generating news releases and stimulating letter writing campaigns.

Lobbying is not a mysterious process that only the specially anointed can successfully master. While the necessary personal relationships and the understanding of legislative procedural nuances don't come immediately, successful lobbying is not that difficult to understand.

In attempting to get a state legislature to support anti-sexual harassment legislation you are actually selling a product. You are trying to convince a group of legislators that eradicating sexual harassment in the schools will benefit them, their constituency, and the state. And like a good salesperson, never take a no as final. If defeated in your attempt this time, begin to prepare for the next year. Thank those who helped you and analyze how you might reach those you were unable to convince this time.

Simply put, to successfully influence your local school board member or state legislator you have to have knowledge of the rules, the people, and the issue, as well as a clear idea of how to put it all together. After that, it takes time, elbow grease, and commitment.

Chapter Seven

Reasons For Hope

There Are Solutions

At the beginning of this book we stated our belief that with effort, education, and training all people can find a better way to live. We've seen evidence that change of the nature required to solve the problem of sexual harassment is possible. According to *How Schools Shortchange Girls,* "A review of research on how books influence children cited 23 studies that demonstrated that books do transmit values to young readers, that multi-cultural readings produce markedly more favorable attitudes toward non-dominant groups than do all-white curricula, that academic achievement for all students was positively correlated with use of nonsexist and multi-cultural materials, and that sex-role stereotyping was reduced in those student whose curriculum portrayed females and males in non-stereotypical roles."

What this says is that change is possible! Sexism, gender bias and sexual harassment can be eradicated. Certainly, it requires effort, but it can be done. And, we have models for change. In a number of places around our country, and in a wide variety of circumstances, change is taking place. This change is occurring as a result of commitment, effort, and education. In this chapter we'll explore some of the models for change.

Writing this book has been a sobering experience. As we interviewed parents, teachers and students we were shocked and disheartened to learn of the extent and severity of sexual harassment in our schools. However, we also found hope and encouragement. All across the country in schools, businesses and even in prisons, we have found there are people who care and are doing something to reduce and eliminate the contentious nature of interactions between males and females.

As we have documented and discussed the trauma of sexual harassment and the failings of many schools and communities to protect our children, we have not meant to imply that educators and parents are universally ignoring the problem. Such is not the case. In fact, there are many examples where tremendous effort has been exerted and significant progress is being made in the fight for gender equity and humane communication across sex lines.

Many teachers, parents, and administrators are dealing with the hard questions and difficult issues surrounding sexual harassment and conflictual relations. We applaud their efforts and urge them to continue. In the pages that follow, we have included an overview of selected programs that we found to be particularly noteworthy. Although these programs are not panaceas, they are inspiring and a great place to start.

"Kindness"

On a beautiful evening in April of 1993, over 700 people crowded into a banquet hall in the Marriott Allis Plaza Hotel in Kansas City. These men, women, and children of all ages were buoyant. They had gathered together to celebrate "kindness." The event was the third annual *Kindness is Contagious ... Catch It* ™ banquet, honoring Kansas City's kindest people. On this Sunday night, three people were to receive the Maxey Dupree Humanitarian Award. The award was inspired by the life and the kindness of Maxey Dupree, a school crossing guard whose friendly smile and never failing wave were, for many years, a Kansas City treasure.

A few days earlier we had the distinct pleasure of meeting Barbara Unell, founder of the *Kindness is Contagious ... Catch It* ™ program. Unell, a respected authority on parenting as well as author and founder of *Twins* magazine, had created the kindness program in response to her growing concern about bullying and peer abuse among children. According to John H. Hoover, associate professor at North Dakota State University and co-author of a 1990 study on bullying, bullying is often a precursor to sexual harassment. According to Unell, "It takes courage for kids to be kind. We want to make the voice of kindness as loud as the voice of violence." The program strives to change attitudes and instill values such as empathy and compassion. Students in over 400 schools in the Kansas City area participate in activities to increase the awareness of their own unkind behaviors and to help develop skills to manage negative feelings. Teachers and administrators say it works.

The impact on students and on the educational process is nothing short of astounding. Students feel safer and more willing to learn. Administrators report a new spirit of support and cooperation among students, teachers, and parents. As the program gains momentum, we fully expect to see even greater increases in academic achievement. The academic success associated with this program happens, in part, because success in school no longer carries punitive peer repercussions. We have great confidence that other destructive behaviors normally associated with educational failure, i.e., teen pregnancy, criminal behavior, drug usage, etc., will diminish.

Kindness is Contagious ...Catch It ™ demonstrates the fallacy of the long accepted dogma that suggests "Kids are always cruel" or "Boys will be boys." Perhaps even more importantly, the kindness program proves that negative social values and behavior can be replaced with positive and productive personal interactions.

The kindness program is based on three goal areas with specific activities suggested for each. The first goal is awareness. The program seeks to increase the students' recognition of how their words and actions impact on others and, ultimately, on themselves. The second goal is skill building. Activities are designed to equip students with effective ways of managing negative feelings and conflict, to assert themselves non-violently, to cope as victims of insensitive peers, and to build satisfying social relationships. The third goal is adult involvement. The program engages and teaches parents and other adults in the process of modeling and supporting kind behavior. Unell said of the kindness program, "It's a symbol of hope." For us, it is more than a symbol of hope, it is proof that we can all learn a better way to live.

"Mutuality"

We're working from the premise that sexual harassment occurs as a flashpoint in the continuum of contentious relations between men and women, boys and girls. And that until we solve the underlying conflict between the sexes, we will continue to live with the pain and suffering of sexual harassment. From the Stone Center for Developmental Services and Studies at Wellesley College, a model for conflict resolution has emerged from the workshops conducted by Janet Surrey and Stephen Bergman. According to the publication entitled *The Woman-Man Relationship: Impasses and Possibilities*, the workshops are "designed to bring men and women together to explore the impact of gender differences in relationships, and to provide a context in which to work toward creating mutuality in male-female relationships."

But, what is mutuality? Surrey and Bergman suggest that "mutuality is a *way* of being in a relationship - a dialogical, open, changing movement in relationship where each person can increasingly represent her or his own experience, feeling, and perceptions, and each can move and be moved by the other and by the relationship." Judith Jordan, writing in *The Meaning of Mutuality* says, "Through empathy and the active interest in the other as a different, complex person, one develops the capacity to first allow the other's differences and ultimately to value and encourage those qualities which make that person different and unique." From Jordan's work we come to understand that mutuality requires some desire or motivation to understand the other person from that person's frame of reference. It involves an ongoing and sustained interest in the inner world of the other. It is an interest in the other person, not simply as someone who will meet our needs, but as a wonderfully unique and inherently valuable individual with whom we can share and grow.

But, why does mutuality matter? It matters because until we achieve the shift to mutuality, no significant progress on difficult issues is possible. Certainly, the contentious relations between men and women (and the sexual harassment that results) are difficult issues. To this point, it doesn't appear that society has made much progress toward the resolution of sexual harassment. Lack of mutuality lies at the very heart of contentious relations between men and women. Lack of mutuality cripples even the most well meaning attempts to eradicate the core causes of sexual harassment. And lack of mutuality prevents boys and men from ever truly understanding the trauma and the terror that girls and women in our society face on a daily basis. Mutuality matters. It matters a great deal.

And, mutuality works. When provoked to a shift to mutuality by the workshops conducted by Surrey and Bergman, people change and problems get solved. Perhaps most startling was the change of behavior among four year old girls and boys in a preschool setting. After having participated in an age appropriate mutuality workshop, boys and girls immediately abandoned previously inviolate rules of play. In virtually every study of the play activity of four year olds (including this group), the dominant reality is separate sex activities. Boys and girls almost never play together. However, after this workshop, girls and boys were running around holding hands, sometimes in a foursome. Almost as remarkable, there was no sign of the hierarchial patterns so predictable among the boys. A single workshop session had dramatically altered the way boys and girls related to one another. Needless to say, the teacher was astonished.

Once again, we can see that change is possible. We can only

guess what incredible benefits might accrue if mutuality training was part and parcel of the educational experience of all young people. Surely, at the very least, we would have constructed a platform from which to address the most serious gender-related conflicts, including sexual harassment. And, quite likely, we would each find our lives and our relationships to be significantly more peaceful and rewarding.

School District Program to Eradicate Sexual Harassment

South Washington County Schools in Cottage Grove, Minnesota is one example of the many school districts that have a long history of working to eradicate sexual harassment. They first adopted their policy prohibiting sexual harassment and sexual violence in 1986. The policy was amended to its present form in 1990. This school district takes sexual harassment very seriously and has done a number of things to implement the policy.

According to Perry Palin, Human Resources Manager for the district, the most important factor in contributing to a successful program of eradicating sexual harassment is the commitment of the school board president, the board as a whole, individual board members, and the superintendent of schools. "Superintendent Dan Hode gives great support to this policy. He and the board expect all staff and students to be trained in sexual harassment issues. Board members have attended employee sexual harassment training to show their support for the programs."

In order to ensure that all people are aware of the policy, it is posted throughout each school. The posting procedure in each building is left to the discretion of the principal, but typically, the principal provides each teacher with a copy of the posting, and asks that it be posted in each classroom. All support employees are also given copies of the policy.

The district also provides inservice opportunities to employees during the school year. Administrators have been trained by an outside consultant who specializes in sexual harassment issues. Some of the larger buildings and departments have also had outside consultants speak to their staffs. Palin personally trained over six hundred employees in 1993. Each year, every employee is scheduled for some orientation to sexual harassment.

All students are also made aware of the district's policy. Again, the specific procedures and time lines are left to the principal of the individual buildings, but principals are directed to have this policy discussed in all classrooms in age-appropriate ways. Some of the elementary principals personally visit the classrooms to do this. Also, in the upper elementary grades, the students are shown a videotape on the differences between good and bad touching which leads to issues of sexual harassment and encourages students to report concerns they have in this area. The secondary health teachers incorporate sexual harassment awareness in their teaching.

In order to ensure that everyone knows exactly what constitutes sexual harassment, all students and staff members are presented with the following specific examples of sexual harassment at school:

Staff-to-Student Harassment

1. A male teacher placing his arms around middle school girls and rubbing their backs as positive reinforcement for a job well done.

2. A teacher's inquiry into a student's personal, social, and sexual life.

3. Leering or staring at the intimate body parts of a student.

4. A bus driver playing a game with elementary students involving tickling and touching of the students by the bus driver.

5. A teacher showing favoritism towards students who welcome sexually suggestive comments or behavior.

Student-to-Student Harassment

1. Student bra snapping, giving "snuggies" or "pantsing" (pulling down boys' or girls' pants or pulling up girls' skirts).

2. Students "rating" other students.

3. Students displaying or circulating centerfolds or sexually explicit materials.

4. Name calling: "slut," "whore," "fag," "lesbian," "cow," or "dog."

5. Teasing students about their sexual activities or lack of sexual activity.

6. Students wearing sexually offensive t-shirts, hats, or pins.

7. Displays of affection between students (i.e. "making out") in the halls.

8. Suggestive comments about apparel.

Student-to-Staff Harassment

1. Students making sexually explicit and threatening comments to a staff member.

2. Students "hiding" sexually explicit materials in a classroom where a teacher will find them.

3.   Students passing around sexually explicit and derogatory illustrations of the principal.

4.   Students making obscene phone calls to a teacher at his or her home.

The South Washington County Schools' policy contains a complaint and investigation procedure. Complaints against students are handled by the building staff. Student discipline may be administered under the student discipline policy. Students have, for example, been removed from school buses for the balance of the school year for sexual harassment incidents on a bus.

Complaints against employees are usually handled by an outside investigator if the complainant is a student, and by the Human Resources Department if the complainant is another employee. Palin's experience is that employees appreciate knowing that they have a way to address these problems, and that their complaints are taken seriously and all parties are treated fairly. This district is confident that sexual harassment has been reduced as a result of a clear policy and fair investigations.

Palin reports that the South Washington County Schools' policy was created to provide a positive working and learning environment, free of sexual harassment. The complaint and investigation procedure provides an opportunity for sexual harassment complaints to be handled quickly, and before they become so serious that they require legal action. Palin is convinced that "the school district and its employees are well treated by this policy, when compared to the costs, delays, notoriety, and stress of going through the courts or other outside agencies."

School Program to Eradicate Sexual Harassment

Goodrich Middle School in Lincoln, Nebraska, is typical of other schools across the country. The behaviors of its students reflect the values of its community. Several years ago a group of school counselors began to observe some male students violating the physical and psychological safety of female students. These behaviors included comments, gestures, inappropriate public displays of affection, and unwelcome touching. The counselors also noticed that many of the female students did not seem to understand their rights to declare and demand respect for personal boundaries.

The counselors determined that students were receiving mixed signals regarding appropriate and inappropriate behavior. Consequently, a team of guidance counselors developed an age appropriate program that addressed a variety of objectives regarding the issue of sexual harassment.

The program includes a discussion of the definition of sexual harassment. This discussion stresses that sexual harassment is sexual behavior that is, "not welcomed, one-sided, and deals with power." The program also stresses that sexual harassment is a violation of the Lincoln Public School Policy.

The program explains that anyone can be sexually harassed. "This means students, teachers, parents, or others who are part of the school (janitors, bus drivers, office or lunch room staff) may be victims of sexual harassment." Students are reminded that although females are most often the victims, males can also be sexually harassed. The training makes a particular point of reminding the students that victims can be from any ethnic or cultural group. However, the program notes that "people of color experience sexual harassment more often than European Americans."

One of the parts of the program that we particularly like is the section where the students are reminded that people make a choice to harass someone. This emphasizes the student's responsibility for his own behavior and reinforces the fact that students have the power to refrain from harassing. Students are reminded that harassers can be male or female, from any ethnic or cultural group, and may be an adult or another student.

The Goodrich program stresses that sexual harassment is not the victim's fault, is not harmless fun, is not normal sexual attraction, and is not "asked for" by the victim. Students are told that sexual harassment usually does not go away if it is ignored, and it usually gets worse if it's not stopped. The presentation concludes by reaffirming that the Lincoln Public Schools will not tolerate sexual harassment and serious consequences will result if a student is found to have sexually harassed another student. The program includes role playing, and question and answer sessions.

According to counselors Cathy Rauch, Luetta Sandquist, and Ann Stokes, there have been "immediate and long term benefits as a result of this program. Everyone now speaks a 'common language' when discussing the issue of sexual harassment. By talking about the 'unspeakable,' students have been given permission to discuss their concerns and to report incidents of sexual harassment."

Although statistics have not been kept, the counselors and administrators believe that there are significantly fewer instances of inappropriate touching and other forms of sexual harassment as a result of this program. When incidents do occur, the counselors have found it helpful to refer to the classroom presentations when talking to students and parents. Valarie Hubbard-Harris, assistant principal at the school, told us, "It is especially important to have this training with seventh grade students because they are still trying out behaviors in an effort to figure out what is appropriate. These kids really never thought about the topic of sexual harassment. They are still carrying some roughhousing behavior of elementary school as they begin to make the transition to secondary school."

Hubbard-Harris reports that because of this program female students are more willing to come into the office and tell the counselors or principal exactly what happened and what they did about it. "For example, an eighth grade girl came to my office this week and said, 'He grabbed my breast and I told him to take his hands off of me. I came in here to report him.' We are seeing much more assertive behaviors on the part of victims of sexual harassment."

Institutional Program for Change

Perhaps the most inspiring and dramatic example of change we've encountered comes from the most surprising and frightening of circumstances. Few situations are as hopeless and violence prone as the world behind the iron gates of a penitentiary. While this book is not intended to address penal reform in any way, we believe the following story can be an inspiration to all. If people in these circumstances can aspire to, and achieve, meaningful change in their lives, surely change is possible in our schools.

Programs for change at the Kansas State Penitentiary and the Kansas Correctional Facility at Lansing can only be described as astonishing. The story begins in 1978 with a survey conceived and conducted by inmates. The survey correlated child abuse with incarceration. At the time, 200 inmates lived in the B Cellblock at the Kansas State Penitentiary (KSP). Of these inmates, 90%

voluntarily participated in the survey. Among the participants, 80% talked openly about being abused as a child. An article in the *Lifers Club Newsletter* reported on the results of the survey.

SuEllen Fried, then president of the National Committee for the Prevention of Child Abuse, happened to see the article. Soon a meeting was arranged between SuEllen and inmates interested in addressing the issues of child abuse and family violence in our society. As a result of that meeting and subsequent efforts, a self-help group called STOP Violence was established within the walls of the Kansas Correctional Facility at Lansing (today known as Lansing Correctional Facility - East). The purpose of the group was to help inmates understand and deal with issues that had previously translated to violent outbursts. Members of the STOP Violence group wanted to change, they wanted to end the cycle of violence that had devastated their lives and the lives of those around them.

Professionals from a diverse range of mental health and self help disciplines provided counseling and training to participants of the group. The group is now self administering and operates in a manner very similar to traditional 12 Step self-help groups on the outside. Success is measured in many different ways. The warden of LCF-East reports that no member of the STOP Violence group has ever been involved in a violent episode within the prison. But, perhaps most telling is one remarkable statistic. Recidivism, or the tendency to return to prison after release, is 14% for participants of the STOP Violence program. This is most startling (and encouraging) when we consider that the recidivism rate of the general prison population is 70%. Given the fact that it costs well over $20,000 annually to keep an inmate incarcerated, STOP Violence is an extremely cost effective program. It is also effective in human terms. The STOP Violence experience has truly made it possible for participants to find a better way to live.

Personal Empowerment Program

One of the most important aspects of sexual harassment prevention is empowerment. Young women must be taught the skills necessary to defend themselves from intimidation and harassment. A number of programs have been developed that empower people to take control of their lives. Personal empowerment programs strive to build self-esteem and personal skills which allow program participants to face problems and interactions in new ways. Men and women who take part in such programs often learn skills to interact with others in a more productive and appropriate manner. For example, women who learn assertiveness often use assertive communication skills and develop an attitude of self-respect ("I have the right to be treated with respect and dignity.") which leads them to stop sexual harassment they encounter, or at least to realize that such behavior is not acceptable. Programs which help men learn to treat others with respect and dignity include communication skills and positive interaction skills. Thus, they learn productive, appropriate, and legal methods of interacting with females. Such programs hold promise for preventing and stopping individual sexual harassment.

Two of the best of these programs were developed by Linda Thurston, and her company, Survival Skills Education and Development, Inc. These two highly successful personal empowerment programs are: *Survival Skills for Women*™ and *Survival Skills for Men.*™ Both programs focus on building self-esteem and respect for others by developing new communication and interaction skills, called basic survival skills. Both programs are presented as a series of ten workshops which were developed to be delivered to intact, single sex groups of 8-15 participants.

This group format for the program promotes a supportive learning environment where all topics and discussions are considered "safe." The individuals of the groups teach and support each other and learn from each others' mistakes and experiences. In addition, research indicates that the individuals provide support to each other and continue their interactions beyond the workshops.

Another positive element of these survival skills programs is the group leader, who is called a Facilitator. The Facilitator is a woman for *Survival Skills for Women™*, and a man for *Survival Skills for Men.™* Thus, the Facilitator provides a positive role model for the participants, as well as serving as a leader of learning activities.

The *Survival Skills for Women™* program's workshop topics are: Assertiveness, Personal Health, Nutrition, Money Management, Child Management, Self-Advocacy, Legal Rights, Coping with Crisis, Community Resources, and Education or Employment. The focus is on developing independence and self-sufficiency through skill development, and a support-group format. This program is being offered in 23 states through organizations such as women's centers, prisons and community corrections, Head Start, human services agencies, and community colleges.

One of the unique aspects of this program is that there is 10 years of research documenting that graduates take control of their lives, design and meet personal and professional goals, and feel less depressed and more empowered. As women learn about their legal rights, and as they learn new communication and assertiveness skills, they also gain the insight that they are in charge of their lives and they deserve to be treated with respect. This empowerment is a first step to preventing or coping with sexual harassment in their lives, and many *Survival Skills for Women*™ graduates have done just that.

Education Can Make A Difference

We have little or no reason to believe that contentious relations between men and women have any genetic or biological foundation. This rather strongly suggests that conflict is socialized or learned. If this is true, then education can be a powerful catalyst for change. However, a change in culture results from a process in which changes of knowledge and beliefs, changes of values and standards, changes of emotional attachments and needs, and changes in the framework of an individual's total life in the group all take place. In other words, the kind of cultural change required to eradicate sexual harassment in our schools requires not just transference of facts, but significant alteration of the belief system of the culture. One of the reasons the Kindness, Mutuality, and Survival Skills models have been so successful is that in the microcosm of those efforts, group values have been significantly altered. In these cases, the group begins to support different values, making it far easier for each individual to accept these new values. Another pillar of success in these programs is the free expression and open discussion of the problematic attitudes or behavior. In order for change to take place, members of the group must feel free to express openly the very sentiments which we are trying to eradicate.

There is no question that resolving the conflict between boys and girls, men and women will require a large component of reeducation. As we have learned in our review of the above programs, there are numerous and varied ways to achieve this reeducation. The purpose of this chapter has not been to mandate specific solutions but to create an awareness that solutions are possible. We also hope the portrayal of the models included in this discussion will lead to even greater exploration and implementation of innovative ideas and programs.

Value of Training

Training is a big part of most of the programs that are being used to help eradicate sexual harassment from our schools. In 1976 Beauvais conducted a study to evaluate the impact of a training program that was designed to increase students' understanding of what constitutes sexual harassment, to increase participants' sensitivity toward students who were sexually harassed, and to reduce tolerance of all participants for sexually harassing behaviors. In this study male and female college students who were resident hall staff members participated in a two hour training session. During this session the participants looked at a series of six videotapes that illustrated various examples of sexual harassment. The students completed a sexual harassment attitude survey prior to and at the completion of the training session. The participants in this study significantly increased their awareness of sexual harassment issues as a result of the training experience. Interestingly, the women participants did not significantly change their perceptions. However, men dramatically increased their recognition of what behavior constitutes sexual harassment and also increased their sensitivity to students who are harassed.

Although changes in attitudes do not necessarily translate into changes in behaviors, a study conducted by Jones and Jacklin reinforced the belief that training can change students' attitudes about sexual harassment. This study indicated that both male and female college students' sexist attitudes were significantly lowered as the result of an introductory course in gender studies.

From the results of these studies, we conclude that training/education efforts can change attitudes and should be begun early in a child's elementary school education.

Recommendations for Eradicating Sexual Harassment

Now that we have discussed the seriousness of the problem of sexual harassment in our schools, and have shared several examples of how various groups are working to develop stronger self-concepts, reduce gender conflict and eradicate sexual harassment from our schools, we would like to offer several additional recommendations. Some of the following recommendations are adapted from a follow-up study on sexual harassment that was conducted by Merit System Protection Board. Others are adapted from suggestions offered by Claire Walsh.

Recommendation #1
Examine The School Environment

A. Examine your school's educational climate with an eye to identifying its hostility to females. Before you begin making policies and rules and regulations you must find out what is going on in your school or school district. Your policy should be responsive to the unique nature of your community, while at the same time ensuring that all students are protected from sexual harassment. Although we have provided several sample policies, we do not recommend that you adopt these or others without carefully examining them.

B. When you are looking at your educational environment, be sure you look at the behavior of teachers, administrators, classified staff, and school board members. As official representatives of the school district, behavior in the teacher's lounge, the golf course, or while attending educational conferences reflects the image and climate of the school district. Professional educators must model non-sexist behavior and eradicate sexual harassment from their own lives.

Recommendation #2
Initiate a Task Force On Sexual Harassment

A. The issue of sexual harassment should not be addressed in a vacuum. Although we can understand why some school administrators are reluctant to discuss this issue with the public, this fear is not well-founded. Sexual harassment is not a school problem. It is a community problem. Each community has a wealth of often untapped resources that can help the school develop appropriate, accurate and effective programs to eradicate sexual harassment. The task force should include representatives from community groups, law enforcement agencies, rape crisis advocates, children's service agencies, and other community organizations, as well as parents, teachers, administrators, and students.

Recommendation #3
Policy Statements

A.   Every school district should have a specific policy statement that prohibits all forms of sexual harassment. In order to be effective, this policy must be widely publicized and detail the specific actions that constitute sexual harassment and define the penalties for each of the actions.

B.   The sexual harassment policy should be annually evaluated, modified if necessary, and reissued. A policy imbedded in a policy manual does little to eradicate harassment or to assist in a defense to charges of sexual harassment.

C.   The policy must make it clear that sexual harassment is against the law and that the school district will not tolerate it.

D.   The policy should be adopted by the board of education and signed by the board president and by the superintendent of schools.

E.   The policy should define the various behaviors that may constitute sexual harassment including a description of activities that may create a hostile environment.

F.   The policy should include the range of penalties the school district can levy against the offender, from warning to dismissal or expulsion. It should also discuss the possibility of personal liability for unlawful acts of harassment.

Recommendation #4
Training

A.   Each school district should tailor their training/education programs to the individual needs of each segment of the school community. For training efforts to succeed, school districts must provide all administrators, teachers, classified staff, students, and parents with more than generic warnings that sexual harassment is improper. All members of the school community must be taught exactly what constitutes sexual harassment and they must be sensitized to understand and recognize what they can do to eradicate sexual harassment.

B.   Training sessions should be developed and presented for parents and other community members.

C.   All employees, students, and parents must be convinced that sexual harassment can be deemed illegal and that strong sanctions can, and will, be applied to any member of the school community who is responsible for such behavior.

D.   All members of the administration, teaching, and support staff should be required to take sexual harassment training. All students should have at least one session in which sexual harassment is defined and the consequences for the harasser and the victim are clearly explained.

E.   The training should thoroughly cover the range of possible behaviors and the circumstances under which those behaviors may be considered sexual harassment, the formal and informal actions for seeking relief, the right to confidentiality under certain circumstance for those alleging harassment, the prohibition of reprisals, and current case law relevant to sexual harassment.

F.   All new employees should receive training early in their employment. All students should receive training early in the school year.

G.   The training program should be periodically evaluated for effectiveness.

H.   Don't separate males from females during training sessions. All employees and all students must receive the same information about this topic. Both males and females have the same rights and responsibilities. By separating them you perpetuate the misconception that most men are guilty of harassment, that only women are victims, and that this is a divisive issue, a battle of the sexes.

Recommendation #5
Complaint and Investigation Procedures

A.   Simply having a sexual harassment policy and training program does not necessarily insulate a school district from liability. In order to be effective, the policy must include a grievance procedure that encourages victims of harassment to come forward.

B.   There should be both a formal and informal avenue of redress available to employees who believe they are victims of sexual harassment. The school district must have a mechanism in place that allows it to quickly institute any needed reforms.

C.   The process should be timely, ensure reasonable confidentiality, and protect the victim from any reprisals. A goal of 120 days to resolve any complaint is reasonable.

Recommendation #6
Enforcement Action

A.   All faculty, staff, and students must clearly understand that the school district has a strong and effective system of sanctions against sexual harassment. They must know that all accusations of sexual harassment will be investigated and if a person is found to be guilty of sexual harassment there will be strong and appropriate penalties.

B.   The school district should publicize the specific information about the penalties harassers face.

Recommendation #7
Additional Prevention Efforts

A.   The school district should conduct periodic, random, anonymous surveys to determine whether sexual harassment is a problem in a given department, building, or classroom.

B.   An evaluation/prevention effort should include conducting periodic follow-up interviews with all personnel involved in the settlement of both informal and formal complaints.

C.   Administrators should assess the current school environment of the employees involved in harassment complaints to ensure that problems relating to that sexual harassment incident no longer exist.

School districts that begin to face and solve the problems of sexual harassment need to be supported by their communities. This process is often painful and may sometimes be embarrassing. New attitudes and behaviors must be developed. Parents must be willing to help their local educators as they create and enforce new policies. It has been our experience that as students and teachers come to understand sexual harassment and trust the school systems' willingness and ability to respond to complaints, there may be an increase in reports of sexual harassment. This is an indication that

178 Sexual Harassment In Our Schools

students trust the school enough to openly address sexual harassment.

Education does not create more harassment. It puts a name on the inappropriate behavior that may already exists. Education does not create more problems for educators. It allows existing problems to be identified and solved at the local level. It is our hope that y joining in partnership with the schools, parent can help the schools eradicate sexual harassment without having to resort to the legal system.

Appendix A
Sample Policies, Forms and Notices

Sample State Statute Against Sexual Harassment

Minnesota Human Rights Act, Minn. Stat. §§363.01-.14 (West 1966 & Supp. 1992)

127.455   MODEL POLICY

The commissioner of education shall maintain and make available to school boards a model sexual harassment and violence policy. The model policy shall address the requirements of section 127.46.

Each school board shall submit to the commissioner of education a copy of the sexual harassment and sexual violence policy the board has adopted.

127.46   SEXUAL HARASSMENT AND VIOLENCE POLICY (Amended 1992)

Each school board shall adopt a written sexual harassment and sexual violence policy that conforms with sections 363.01 to 363.15. The policy shall apply to pupils, teachers, administrators, and other school personnel, include reporting procedures, and set forth disciplinary actions that will be taken for violation of the policy. Disciplinary actions must conform with collective bargaining agreements and sections 127.27 to 127.39. The policy must be conspicuously posted throughout each school building and included in each school's student handbook on school policies. Each school must develop a process for discussing the school's sexual harassment and violence policy with students and school employees.

(After reviewing the statutes of each state and the District of Columbia, we choose the statute from Minnesota as an example of a comprehensive state statute.)

Sample School District Policy

Sexual Harassment And Sexual Violence Policy

I. General Policy

Sexual harassment is a form of discrimination prohibited by Title VII of the Civil Rights Act of 1964 and Title IX of the Education Amendments of 1972. Sexual harassment is any unwanted attention of a sexual nature. Sexual violence is a physical act of aggression that includes a sexual act or sexual purpose.

(Your School's Name) is committed to maintaining a learning environment that is free from sexual harassment and sexual violence, where all employees and students can work and study together comfortably and productively. The School District prohibits any form of sexual harassment or sexual violence.

It shall be a violation of this policy for any student or employee of **(Your School's Name)** to harass a student or an employee through conduct or communication of a sexual nature as defined by this policy. It shall be a violation of this policy for any student or employee of **(Your School's Name)** to be sexually violent to a student or employee.

The School District will act to investigate all complaints, either formal or informal, verbal or written, of sexual harassment or sexual violence and to discipline any student or employee who sexually harasses or is sexually violent to a student or employee of the School District.

II. Definition of Sexual Harassment and Sexual Violence

Sexual harassment consists of unwelcome sexual advances, requests for sexual favors, sexually motivated physical conduct or other verbal or physical conduct or communication of a sexual nature when:

1.   Submission to such conduct is made either explicitly or implicitly a term or condition of an individual's employment, or of obtaining an education; or

2.   Submission to or rejection of that conduct or communication by an individual is used as a factor in decisions affecting that individual's employment or education; or

3.   The conduct or communication has the purpose or effect of substantially or unreasonably interfering with an individual's work employment or education, or creating an intimidating, hostile, or offensive employment or eduction environment.

Examples of prohibited behavior that is sexual in nature and is unsolicited and unwelcome include:

•   **Written Contact**--sexually suggestive or obscene letters, notes, invitations, drawings. This also includes computer terminal messages of a sexual nature.

•   **Verbal Contact**--sexually suggestive or obscene comments, threats, jokes (including jokes about racial and gender-specific traits), any sexual propositions, comments about an employee's body or sexual characteristics that are used in a negative or embarrassing way.

•   **Physical Contact**--any intentional pats, squeezes, touching, pinching, repeatedly brushing up against another's body, assault, blocking movement, or coercing sexual intercourse.

•   **Visual Contact**--suggestive looks, leering, or staring at another's body, gesturing, displaying sexually suggestive objects or pictures, cartoons, posters or magazines.

•   **Sexual Blackmail**--Sexual behavior to control another employee's work environment is also prohibited--this includes salary, promotions, evaluations and/or better job assignments or grades.

Every effort will be made to eliminate sexual harassment by non-employees including parents, suppliers, and other visitors to the school.

III. Reporting Procedures

Any person who believes he or she has been the victim of sexual harassment by a student or an employee of the School District, or any person with knowledge or belief of conduct which may constitute sexual harassment or sexual violence, should report the alleged acts immediately to an appropriate School District official as designated by this policy. The School District encourages the reporting party or complainant to make his or her report in writing.

A.   **In Each School Building.** The building principal is the person responsible for receiving oral or written reports of sexual harassment or sexual violence at the building level. Upon receipt of a report, the principal must notify the Manager of Human Resources immediately without screening or investigating the report. A written report will be forwarded simultaneously to the Manager of Human Resources. If the report is given verbally, the principal shall reduce it to written form within 24 hours and forward it to the Manager of Human Resources. Failure to forward any sexual harassment or sexual violence report or complaint as provided herein will result in disciplinary action. If the complaint involves the building principal the complaint shall be filed directly with the Manager of Human Resources.

B.   **District-Wide.** The School Board hereby designates the Manager of Human Resources to receive reports or complaints of sexual harassment and sexual violence from any individual, employee or victim of sexual harassment or sexual violence and also from the building principals as outlined above. If the complaint involves the Manager of Human Resources, the complaint shall be filed directly with the Superintendent. If the complaint involves the Superintendent, the complaint shall be filed with the Manager of Human Resources, who shall report the complaint to the Chair of the School Board.

The School District shall conspicuously post the name of the Manager of Human Resources, including a mailing address and telephone number.

C.   Submission of a complaint or report of sexual harassment or sexual violence will not affect the individual's future employment, grades, or work assignments.

D.   Use of written complaints is not mandatory. The School District will respect the confidentiality of the complainant and the individual(s) against whom the complaint is filed, as much as possible, consistent with the School District's legal obligations and the necessity to investigate allegations of sexual harassment and sexual violence and take disciplinary action when the conduct has occurred.

IV. Investigation and Recommendation

By authority of the School District, the Manager of Human Resources, upon receipt of a report or complaint alleging sexual harassment or sexual violence, shall immediately authorize an investigation. This investigation may be conducted by School District officials or by a third party designated by the School District. The investigating party shall provide a written report of the status of the investigation within 10 working days to the Superintendent of Schools and the Manager of Human Resources.

In determining whether the alleged conduct constitutes sexual harassment or sexual violence, the School District should consider the surrounding circumstances, the nature of the sexual advances, relationships between parties involved, and the context in which the alleged incidents occurred. Whether a particular action or incident constitutes sexual harassment or sexual violence requires a determination based on all the facts and the surrounding circumstances.

The investigation may consist of personal interviews with the complainant, the individual(s) against whom the complaint is filed, and others who have knowledge of the alleged incident(s) or circumstances giving rise to the complaint. The investigation may also consist of any other methods and documents deemed pertinent by the investigator.

In addition, the School District may take immediate steps, at its discretion, to protect the complainant, students, and employees pending the completion of an investigation of alleged sexual harassment or sexual violence.

The Manager of Human Resources shall make a report to the Superintendent upon completion of the investigation.

V. School District Action

A.   Upon receipt of a recommendation that the complaint is valid, the District will take such action, as appropriate, based on the results of the investigation.

B.   The result of the investigation of each complaint filed under these procedures will be reported in writing to the complainant by the School District. The report will document any disciplinary action taken as a result of the complaint.

VI. Reprisal

The School District will discipline any individual who retaliates against any person who reports alleged sexual harassment or sexual violence or retaliates against any person who testifies, assists, or participates in an investigation proceeding or hearing relating to a sexual harassment or sexual violence complaint. Retaliation includes, but is not limited to, any form of intimidation, reprisal, or harassment.

VII. Right to Alternative Complaint Procedures

These procedures do not deny the right of any individual to pursue other avenues of recourse which may include filing charges with the State Department of Human Rights, initiating civil action, or seeking redress under state criminal statutes and or federal law.

VIII. Sexual Harassment or Sexual Violence as Sexual Abuse

(Under certain circumstances, sexual harassment or sexual violence may constitute sexual abuse under state statutes. In such situations School Districts shall comply with their state reporting procedures.) Nothing in this policy will prohibit the School District from taking immediate action to protect victims of alleged sexual abuse.

IX. Discipline

Any School District action taken pursuant to this policy will be consistent with requirements of applicable collective bargaining agreements, State and District policies. The School District will take such disciplinary action it deems necessary and appropriate, including warning, suspension or immediate discharge, or expulsion, in the case of a student, to end sexual harassment and sexual violence and prevent its recurrence.

X .   Training

Training is the key in establishing a prevention plan for sexual harassment. Yearly training sessions for all employees and students concerning rights and legal options will be established. New employee orientation sessions will include training in sexual harassment. Administrators and teachers will be trained in how to keep the school free from sexual harassment and how to handle sexual harassment complaints.

(After reviewing scores of school district sexual harassment policies, we choose the policy from South Washington County Schools, Cottage Grove, Minnesota as the basis for our model policy. Although we have modified their policy by adding material from other policies, it is still interesting to compare this policy to the Minnesota Statute on Sexual Harassment. The South Washington County Schools policy was revised in November of 1990.)

Sample Sexual Harassment Notice

"Your School District's Name"

PROHIBITS

Sexual Harassment

Sexual Harassment
is a form of discrimination
prohibited by Title IX of the Education Amendments
of 1972.

Sexual harassment is any unwanted
attention of a sexual nature.

Incidents of sexual harassment
should be reported to **"NAME OF PERSON."**
To report incidents, call:

000-0000

"Your School's Name"

Sample Letter to Harasser

Date

John Doe
XYZ School
City, State   00000

Mr. Doe:

On November 1, 1993 you asked me out and made comments about my body and clothing saying "you would look better in short skirts." I told you that I was not interested in a social relationship and I didn't like your comments about my clothes or body.

Today as I passed you in the hallway, you brushed up against me and asked me to meet you after school. When I turned and walked away you patted me on the buttocks. This was a very embarrassing situation because several other students observed this behavior.

I have no interest in a social relationship and your persistent comments about my clothing, my body, touching me, and meeting you socially are very upsetting to me. I do not want any personal relationship with you.

I have attached our school's policy on sexual harassment. The behavior that I have described is a clear violation of our policy and is also illegal under federal law.

If you continue in this behavior, I will take action at once by taking this letter with me when I discuss this matter with the principal.

Sincerely,

Sexual Harassment Complaint Form

Name:_____

Date:_____

Department:_____

Who was responsible for the
harassment?_____

Describe the sexual harassment.

_____
_____
_____
_____

Date, time, and place the harassment occurred.

_____
_____

Were there other employees or students involved with the
harassment?

_____

If so, who was responsible and describe their involvement.

_____
_____
_____

List any witnesses to the harassment.

_____
_____

What was your reaction to the harassment?

_____
_____

Describe any subsequent incidents.

_____
_____
_____

_____
Signature of Complainant

Appendix B
A Summary of EEOC Guidelines

SEC. 1604.11 Sexual Harassment

(a) Harassment on the basis of sex is a violation of Sec. 703 of Title VII. Unwelcome sexual advances, requests for sexual favors, and other verbal or physical conduct of a sexual nature constitute sexual harassment when (1) submission to such conduct is made either explicitly or implicitly a term or condition of an individual's employment, (2) submission to or rejection of such conduct by an individual is used as the basis for employment decisions affecting such individual, or (3) such conduct has the purpose or effect of unreasonably interfering with an individual's work performance or creating an intimidating, hostile, or offensive working environment.

(b) In determining whether alleged conduct constitutes sexual harassment, the Commission will look at the record as a whole and the totality of the circumstances, such as the nature of the sexual advances and the context in which the alleged incidents occurred. The determination of the legality of a particular action will be made from the facts, on a case by case basis.

(c) Applying general Title VII principles, an employer, employment agency, joint apprenticeship committee or labor organization (hereinafter collectively referred to as "employer") is responsible for its acts and those of its agents and supervisory employees with respect to sexual harassment regardless of whether the specific acts complained of were authorized or even forbidden by the employer and regardless of whether the employer knew or should have known of this occurrence. The Commission will examine the circumstances of the particular employment relationship and the job functions performed by the individual in determining whether an individual acts in either a supervisory or agency capacity.

(d) With respect to conduct between fellow employees, an employer is responsible for acts of sexual harassment in the workplace where the employer (or its agents or supervisory employees) knows or should have known of the conduct, unless it can show that it took immediate and appropriate corrective action.

(e) An employer may also be responsible for the acts of non-employees, with respect to sexual harassment of employees in the workplace, where the employer (or its agents or supervisory employees) knows or should have known of the conduct and fails to take immediate and appropriate corrective action. In reviewing these cases the Commission will consider the extent of the employer's control and any other legal responsibility which the employer may have with respect to the conduct of such non-employees.

(f) Prevention is the best tool for the elimination of sexual harassment. An employer should take all steps necessary to prevent sexual harassment from occurring, such as affirmatively raising the subject, expressing strong disapproval, developing appropriate sanctions, informing employees of their right to raise, and how to raise, the issue of harassment under Title VII, and developing methods to sensitize all concerned.

(g) Other related practices: Where employment opportunities or benefits are granted because of an individual's submission to the employer's requests for sexual favors, the employer may be held liable for unlawful sex discrimination against other persons who were qualified for but denied that employment opportunity or benefit. [Section 1604.11 reads as last amended by 45 FR 74676, effective November 10, 1980]

Appendix C
Selected Cases In The Legal History of Sexual Harassment

1972

N. Jay Rogers v. EEOC, 454 F.2d 234 (5th Cir. 1971). cert. denied, 406 U.S. 957 (1972).
The hostile work environment theory was first presented in this case. A Spanish surnamed woman charged that her work environment was so heavily polluted with discrimination as to destroy the emotional and psychological stability of all minority group workers. The court acknowledged that an individual's well-being could be undermined by a series of complex and persuasive activities.

Connon v. University of Chicago, 441 U.S. 677 (1979).
In this case the U.S. Supreme Court held that a student had an implied right of action for discrimination under Title IX of the Education Amendments of 1972. Title IX bars discrimination in educational programs that receive federal funds.

1978

Heelan v. Johns-Manville Corp., 451 F. Supp. 1382 (D.Colo. 1978).
An employee who refused to have sex with a supervisor was terminated. The court ruled that an employer can be relieved of liability for harassment by a supervisor only if the employer 1) had a policy of discouraging harassment, 2) the employee failed to present the matter to a publicized grievance board, and 3) the employer failed to rectify the situation.

1981

EEOC v. Sage Realty Corp., 507 F. Supp. 599 (S.D. N.Y. 1981).
A lobby attendant was discharged for refusing to wear a revealing bicentennial uniform. The building management corporation and its cleaning contractor were held jointly liable for sex discrimination in violation of Title VII.

Bundy v. Jackson. 641 F.2d 934 (D.C.Cir. 1981).
Sexual harassment may amount to discrimination even if there is no loss of tangible job benefits. An employer is responsible

for discriminatory acts of its agents or supervisors regardless of whether the employer knew or should have know of the acts, but may negate liability by taking immediate and appropriate corrective action.

1982

Gan v. Kepro Circuit Systems, 28 FEP Cases 639 (E.D. Mo. 1982).

The court ruled that a female employee who regularly used vulgar language, initiated sexually oriented conversations with counselors, asked male employees about their sex lives, and discussed her own marital sexual relations, was not constructively discharged. The court ruled that she had contributed to the distasteful working environment by her own conduct and in fact welcomed the conduct.

1983

Barrnett v. Omaha National Bank, 584 F. Supp. 22 (D.Neb. 1983).

Because of the Bank's remedial response to a female employee's complaint of her male co-worker's inappropriate behavior on a business trip, the claim against the bank failed. The bank launched an investigation within four days. The perpetrator was placed on 90 day probation, warned that future misconduct would result in termination, and was passed by for pay raises for 15 months. A letter reporting the incident was placed in his personnel file. For failing to intervene, another male employee was reprimanded, passed over at least three times for promotions, and denied raises for 18 months. A letter was also placed in his file.

Cummings v. Walsh Construction Co., 561 F. Supp. 872 (S.D. Ga. 1983).

A female employee who rebuffed advances of supervisors was required to perform harsh and unpleasant tasks. Sexual harassment was so widespread that the company had constructive knowledge of it; top level management personnel were involved in the activity, therefore the company was liable for the activity even though the company policy was violated.

Katz v. Dole,700 F. 2d 251, 31 FEP Cases 1521, 1524 (4th Cir. 1983).

In this case the court noted that, since any act of sexual harassment was "an intentional assault on an individual's innermost privacy," once the plaintiff proves that the harassment took place, "the most difficult legal question will concern the responsibility of the employer for that harassment."

1985

Horn v. Duke Homes, 755 F.2d 599 (7th Cir. 1985).

The corporation was held strictly liable under doctrine of *respondeat superior* where a plant supervisor used his authority to hire and fire employees and to extort sex from female employees in exchange for keeping their jobs.

King v. Palmer, 778 F.2d 878 (D.C. Cir. 1985).

The concept of sexual favoritism as a category of sexual harassment was presented when an employee who established that a sexual relationship between her supervisor and another employee influenced that employee promotion over her was not required to prove the sexual relationship had been consummated.

Boyd v. Hayes Living Health Care Agency, 44 FEP Cases 332 (W.D. Tenn. 1985).

Even though the administrator did not expressly invite her to have a sexual relationship or force one on her, the court ruled that a female employee was sexually harassed by an administrator, when he insisted that she come to his hotel room, offered her wine, tried to get her to look at a sexually explicit movie and magazines, attempted to restrain her departure, and slammed the door in anger when she left.

Harrison v. Reed Rubber Co., 603 F.Supp. 1457 (E.D.Mo. 1985).

A factory line worker was demoted after complaining of her superintendent's open and unwelcome affection for her. Instructions to plant supervisors to stay away from an employee, without directions to cease harassment and without monitoring by the employer, were not enough to preclude employer liability.

Downes v. FAA, 775 F.2d 288 (Fed.Cir. 1985).

Five incidents of sexually offensive conduct in three years did not establish a pattern sufficient to constitute a pervasively hostile environment.

1986

Moylan v. Maries County, 792 F.2d 746 (8th Cir. 1986).

The Eighth Circuit held that a sexually hostile work environment constituted a violation of Title VII.

Meritor Savings Bank v. Vinson, 447 U.S. 57, (1986).

The U.S. Supreme Court recognized sexual harassment as a prohibited act under Title VII of the Civil Rights Act of 1964. "Without question, when a supervisor sexually harasses a subordinate because of a subordinate's sex, that supervisor discriminates on the basis of sex." In this case the Court found a legal violation even though the victim did not report the harassment nor utilize the existing grievance procedure. The court held that lack of knowledge of the harassment will not automatically shield the employer from liability.

Rabidue v. Oscela Refining Co., 805 F.2d 611 (6th Cir. 1986).

The court ruled that Title VII was not designed to bring about a transformation in the social mores of American workers. The court held that maintaining a hostile or abusive working environment "must interfere with the job performance of a reasonable person in order for the behavior to be determined sexual harassment." This case is interesting because the "reasonable woman test" was first set out in Judge Drupansky's dissent.

Moire v. Temple University School of Medicine, 613 F. Supp. 1360 (E.D. Pa. 1985, aff'd 800 F. 2d 1136 (3d Cir. 1986).

In this case the court stated that sexual harassment "demeans and degrades women." The court held that "abusive environment sexual harassment" was an actionable form of sexual harassment, and occurs where multiple incidents of offensive conduct lead to an environment violative of a victim's civil rights.

Scott v. Sears, Roebuck & Co., 605 F. Supp 1047, 37 FEP Cases 878 (N.D.Ill, 1986, affirmed 798 F.2d 210, 41 FEP 805 (7th Cir. 1986).

Because co-workers do not have the power over a fellow employee to create a *quid pro quo* situation, the employer is liable for the actions of employees under EEOC guidelines "where the employer knows or should have known of the conduct, unless it can be shown that it took immediate and appropriate corrective action."

1987

Shaw v. Nebraska Department of Correctional Services, 666 F.Supp. 1330, (1987).

Male members of the promotion selection committee created a "sexist" environment by referring to the females as "girls," "honey," and "dear." In its holding the court implied that the correctional facility was required to eliminate the "sexist" environment.

1988

Lipsett v. University of Puerto Rico, 864 F.2d 881 (1st Cir. 1988).

This decision affirmed the definition in Rabidue of what constitutes a hostile or abusive working environment. However, "unless the fact finder keeps both the man's and the woman's perspective in mind the courts may be too ready to accept the offender's behavior as reasonable." This case also found that Title IX of the 1972 Education Amendments covers sexual harassment in a similar manner to Title VII's coverage. The court held that Title IX prohibits sexual harassment when it affects "tangible aspects" of employment or education, or is so "severe and pervasive" that it alters the work or education environment.

Lewellyn v. Celanese Corp, 693 (W.D.N.Y. 1988).

In this case a female truck driver received frequent threats and sexual solicitations from her coworkers. The coworkers had established a "club" to see which one would have sex with her. She complained to management, got nowhere, and eventually quit to seek medical attention after a male coworker exposed himself to her in the rest room. A federal court said that she had been "constructively discharged" and it is the same as an illegal firing.

Broderick v. Ruder, 46 FEP Cases 1272 (D.D.C. 1988).

A female employee was forced to work in an environment in which managers harassed her, and other female employees, by bestowing preferential treatment upon those who submitted to their sexual advances. The court ruled that consensual sexual relations among employees in exchange for tangible employment benefits can create a sexually hostile working environment for other employees.

Bennett v. Corroon & Black Corp., 845 F. 2d 104, 46 EDP P. 37, 955, 46 FEP Cases 1329 (5th Cir. 1988).

A female employee alleged sexual harassment where she was depicted in cartoons in the men's rest room engaging in crude and deviant sexual activities. Although the Court of Appeals concluded that the conduct in question constituted sexual harassment, it concluded that, because the employer had immediately changed management upon learning of the allegation and had continued to pay the employee her salary until she found another job, she was not entitled to further relief.

Karen Smith v. Hennepin Technical Center, et. al. 1988 WL 53400 (D.Minn.).

In this case students continuously complained to administrators about incidents of sexual harassment. The Court held that Hennepin Technical Center administrators should have know of the harassment and should have acted to stop and correct the harassment.

1989

Price Waterhouse v. Hopkins, 57LS 1165 (U.S. Supreme Court, May 1, (1989).

In this Title VII sex discrimination case, the Court held that when an employee has shown an employer's unlawful motive was involved in an employment decision, the burden of proof shifts to the employer to prove by a preponderance of the evidence that it would have taken the same action without regard to the unlawful motive. The Court agreed that sex stereotyping, such as was practiced by the accounting firm, violated Title VII. The preponderance of evidence test means that an employer must show only that more evidence than not is on its side.

Stoneking v. Bradford Area School Dist., 882 F.2d 720 (3rd Cir. 1989).

In this case, a male band director coerced a female high school student into engaging in various sexual acts with him on school grounds by physical force and threats. The school district had ignored complaints from other students whom the band director had previously attacked. The court ruled that the principal and assistant principal were not entitled to qualified immunity from liability where they maintained a policy, practice or custom of failing to take action on students' complaints of sexual misconduct by teachers, which created a "climate that facilitated sexual abuse of students by teachers in general."

Fisher v. Tacoma School Dist. No. 10, 53 Wash. App. 591, 769 P.2d 318 (1989).

A female assistant custodian of a high school filed suit against the chief custodian for sexual harassment which involved, among other incidents, leaving an anonymous note on the custodians' lunch table that stated, "Discrimination is hard to prove."

1990

King v. Board of Regents University of Wis., 898 F.2d 522 (7th Cir. 1990).

A female assistant professor filed suit against a male assistant dean who had subjected her to suggestive innuendos, suggestive leering, offensive sexual touching, forcible kissing, and insistence that he "have her" in front of others. The federal court of appeals held that sexual harassment of public employees may violate the Fourteenth Amendment's Equal Protection Clause.

1991

Ellison v. Brady, 924 F.2d 872 (9th Cir. 1991).

In this case, the court established the "reasonable woman" standard. The court stated that, "Many women share common concerns which men do not necessarily share. For example, because women are disproportionately victims of rape and sexual assault, women have a stronger incentive to be concerned with sexual behavior. Women who are victims of mild forms of sexual harassment may understandably worry whether a harasser's conduct is merely a prelude to violent sexual assault. Men, who are rarely victims of sexual assault, may view sexual conduct in a vacuum without a full appreciation of the social setting of the underlying threat of violence that a woman may perceive."

Robinson v. Jacksonville Shipyards, 760 F.Supp. 1486 (M.D.Fla. 1991).

In this case, the court ruled that nude pin-ups in the workplace is sexual harassment. Robinson testified that pornographic pictures were displayed at 40 sites in the Jacksonville Shipyards and she found them offensive. The Robinson court took the case one step further by establishing that the pornographic pictures had a direct affect on working conditions. Male coworkers made suggestive remarks to her when they were in the presence of the pornographic pictures. When she objected to the pictures, the sexual taunting increased, thus creating a hostile and intimidating working environment. The court ruled that even though some female employees did not complain of the work environment or find some behaviors objectionable, the fact that a "reasonable woman" would find that the working environment was abusive was sufficient to cause the court to rule in favor of the plaintiff.

Monohon v. Sullivan Payne Co. (Iowa Dist. Ct., Polk Cty., No. 70-41225, Novak, J., 6/12/91).

A female vice-president who was forced to resign because of sexual harassment was awarded $6.3 million from a former employer.

1992

Franklin v. Gwinnett County, GA Public Schools , 117 L. Ed 2d 209 (1992).

In this the U. S. Supreme Court granted certiorari to review a Title IX claim brought by a high school student against a school district employee and the school district. The Court ruled that students who claim they were sexually harassed may seek monetary damages, in addition to other remedies, when they sue that school and/or school officials. In this case, a female high school student filed a suit against a school district for sexual harassment by her teacher. The teacher, at first, gave the student special attention. He later followed her at school. Finally, he excused her from class and had sexual intercourse with her on school grounds. School officials were aware of this situation. The teacher resigned and all matters against him were dropped. Prior to this case, Title IX was thought to provide only injunctive relief to stop discriminatory practices.

Jane Doe v. Taylor I.S.D. 975 F.2d 137 (5th Cir. 1992).

The 5th Circuit has recently held that a student has a constitutional right to be free from sexual molestation by a state employed school teacher and that the superintendent and principal have an affirmative duty to protect a student from such an intrusion.

Appendix D
Gender Equity Resources

Alabama
Ann Turnham Smith
State Department of Education
State Office Building, Room 812
4505 Executive Park Dr.
Montgomery, Alabama 36116
205-242-7900 (ph)
205-279-6779 (fax)

Mae Willa Mason
Sex Equity Coordinator
State Department of Education
Gordon Persons Building
Room 5233
50 N. Ripley Street
Montgomery, AL 36130
205-242-9115 (ph)
205-279-9708 (fax)

Alaska
Naomi Stockdale
Sex Equity Coordinator
Goldbelt Building
Pouch F - Alaska Office Bldg.
Juneau, AK 99811
907-465-4685 (ph)
907-465-3436 (fax)

Arizona
Jenny Erwin, Specialist
Equal Vocational Opportunities
State Department of Education
1535 West Jefferson St.
Phoenix, AZ 85007
602-542-5357 (ph)
602-542-1849 (fax)

Arkansas
Edith (Cooper) Ehrmann
Supervisor
Sex Equity Program

Luther Hardin Bldg.
Room 307
#3 Capitol Mall
Little Rock, AR 72201-1083
501-682-1502 (ph)
501-682-1509 (fax)

California
Connie Gipson
State Department of Education
1507 21st Street, Suite 109
Sacramento, CA 95814
916-323-3481 (ph)

Colorado
Carol Vote
Sex Equity Specialist
Colorado Community College
Parkway Center, Suite 600
1391 North Spear Boulevard
Denver, CO 80204-2554
303-620-4068 (ph)
303-825-4295 (fax)

Connecticut
Diana Woolis
Vocational Equity Consultant
Division of Vocational Equity
Technical and Adult Education
25 Industrial Park Rd.
Middletown, CT 06457
203-638-4190 (ph)
203-632-1854 (fax)

Delaware
Carol Psaros
State Supervisor
State Department of Education
Townsend Building
PO Box 1402
Dover, DE 19903

302-739-4681 (ph)
302-739-3092 (fax)

District of Columbia
Eunice Wright Jones
Sex Equity Coordinator
Division of Vocational Education
415 Twelfth Street N.W.
Suite 1004
Washington, DC 20004
202-727-1037 (ph)
202-724-5307 (fax)

Florida
Charlotte Carney Gore
Equity Administration Office
Florida Education Center
Room 1124
Tallahassee, FL 32399-0400
904-922-5790 (ph)
904-487-0419 (fax)

Georgia
Billy Tidwell
Coordinator, Vocational Equity
Office of Vocational Equity
1862 Twin Towers East
Atlanta, GA 30334
404-656-6561 (ph)
404-651-8984 (fax)

Guam
Micki L. Lonsdale
Program Specialist
Women's Resource Center
Guam Community College
PO Box 23069
GMF, Guam 96921-0307
671-734-8330 (fax)

Hawaii
Barbara Tavares
Coordinator
Sex Equity
Department of Education

2302 Ahe Street
A-206
Honolulu, HI 96816
808-737-5522 (ph)
808-737-5524 (fax)

Idaho
Shirley Silver
Vocational Education Equity
State Department of Education
Len B. Jordan Building
650 W. State Street
Boise, ID 83720
208-334-3216 (ph)
208-334-2365 (fax)

Illinois
Joe Turek
Sex Equity Supervisor
Illinois State Department of
Education
DAVTE, E-426
100 North First Street
Springfield, IL 62777
217-782-4620 (ph)
217-782-0679 (fax)

Indiana
Jean Person, Director
Access & Equity
Commission on Vocational and
Technical Education
IGCS-E204
10 North Senate Street
Indianapolis, IN 46204-2277
317-232-1823 (ph)
317-232-1815 (fax)

Iowa
Mary Wiberg
Sex Equity Coordinator
State Department of Education
Grimes State Office Bldg.
Des Moines, IA 50319
515-281-8584 (ph)

515-242-5988 (fax)

Kansas
Cheryl Brown Henderson
Program Specialist
Vocational Equity
State Department of Education
120 East 10th Street
Topeka, KS 66612
913-296-2078 (ph)
913-296-7933 (fax)

Kentucky
Bettie Tipton, Director
Equal Vocational Opportunity
Dept. of Adult & Technical Education
2014 Capitol Plaza Tower
500 Mero Street
Frankfort, KY 40601
502-564-3662 (ph)
502-564-5316 (fax)

Louisiana
Joy Joseph, Supervisor
Sex Equity
Office of Vocational Education
State Department of Education
PO Box 44064
Baton Rouge, LA 70804
504-342-3534 (ph)
504-342-7856 (fax)

Maine
Edward Maroon
Education Specialist
State House Station 23
Augusta, ME 04333
207-289-5854 (ph)
207-289-5894 (fax)

Maryland
June Wilson
Vocational Equity Specialist
Vocational Education Division
State Department of Education

200 W. Baltimore Street
Baltimore, MD 20201-2595
301-333-2079 (ph)
301-333-2099 (fax)

Massachusetts
Sex Equity Coordinator
State Department of Education
Quincy Center Plaza
1385 Hancock Street
Quincy, MA 02169
617-770-7356 (ph)
617-770-7605 (fax)

Michigan
Sherry Anderson
Single Parent/Homemaker
Coordinator
Michigan Department of Education
PO Box 30008
Lansing, MI 48909
517-373-3361 (ph)
517-373-2759 (fax)

Minnesota
Shirley Walker, Equity Manager
Rm 365, Capitol Square Building
550 Cedar Street
St. Paul, MN 55101
612-297-1484 (ph)
612-296-4217 (fax)

Mississippi
Amy Janous
Sex Equity Coordinator
State Department of Education
PO Box 771
Jackson, MS 39205
601-359-3957 (ph)
601-359-2326 (fax)

Missouri
Georganna Beachboard
Director, Special Vocational Services
State Department of Education

PO Box 480
Jefferson City, MO 65101
314-751-2661 (ph)
314-751-1179 (fax)

Montana
Jane Karas
Gender Equity Coordinator
33 S. Last Chance Gulch
Helena, MT 59620-2602
406-444-5950 (ph)
406-444-7729 (fax)

Nebraska
Sharon Katt
State Coordinator
Vocational Equity Program
Box 94987
301 Centennial Mall South
Lincoln, NE 68509-4987
402-471-2405 (ph)
402-471-2701 (fax)

Nevada
Carole Gribble
State Department of Education
Vocational Education
400 King Street
Carson City, NV 89701
702-687-3144 (ph)
702-687-5660 (fax)

New Hampshire
Nishma Duffy
Consultant in Equal Access Education
Bureau of Vo-Tech Education
101 Pleasant Street
Concord, NH 03301
603-271-3186 (ph)
603-271-1953 (fax)

New Jersey
Patricia Mitchel
Sex Equity Coordinator
State Department of Education

Office of Women in Equal Access
Voc. Ed.
225 W. State Street CN 500
Trenton, NJ 08625
609-292-6580 (ph)
609-633-0658 (fax)

New Mexico
Sharon Fox
State Supervisor, Equal Vocational
Opportunity
State Education Building
300 Don Gaspar
Santa Fe, NM 87501-2786
505-827-6646 (ph)
505-828-6696 (fax)

New York
Mary Ann Etu, Supervisor
Occupational Education Equity
New York State Education
Department
5D45 CEC
OCP-BOCEPS
Albany, NY 12230
518-474-3973 (ph)
518-486-4760 (fax)

North Carolina
Doris Jacobs
Department of Community Colleges
200 W. Jones Street
Raleigh, NC 27603-1337
919-733-7051 (ph)
919-733-0680 (fax)

North Dakota
Janet Placek, Coordinator
North Dakota State Board for
Vocational Education
State Capitol Building, 15th Floor
600 East Boulevard Avenue
Bismarck, ND 58505-0610
701-224-2678 (ph)
701-224-3000 (fax)

Ohio
Connie Blair
Sex Equity Supervisor
Division of Vocational Education
65 South Front Street, Room 909
Columbus, OH 43266-0308
614-644-5910 (ph)
614-644-5702 (fax)

Oklahoma
Lou Ann Hargrave, Director
State Department of Voc. and Tech.
Education
Educational Equity Services
1500 W. 7th Avenue
Stillwater, OK 74074
405-743-5128 (ph)
405-743-5142 (fax)

Oregon
Hilda Thompson, Specialist
State Department of Education
Vocational Equal Education
Opportunity
700 Pringle Parkway, S.E.
Salem, OR 97310-0290
503-378-2182 (ph)
503-378-8434 (fax)

Pennsylvania
Jayne M. Acri
Sex Equity Coordinator
State Department of Education
333 Market Street
Harrisburg, PA 17126
717-787-5293 (ph)
717-783-6672 (fax)

Puerto Rico
Sara Velazquez
Sex Equity Liaison
Department of Education
PO Box 759
Hato Rey, PR 00919
809-758-4919 (ph)

Rhode Island
Linda Greenwood
Sex Equity Consultant
State Department of Education
Bureau of Vocational and Adult Ed.
22 Hayes Street
Providence, RI 02809
401-277-2705 (ph)
401-277-6178 (fax)

South Carolina
Consultant in Sex Equity
State Department of Education
912-C Rutledge Building
Columbia, SC 29201
803-734-8451 (ph)
803-734-8624 (fax)

South Dakota
Amy Sneller Orwick
State Supervisor
Sex Equity
State Department of Education
Office for Vocational Education
700 Governors Drive
Pierre, SD 57501
605-773-3423 (ph)
605-773-6139 (fax)

Tennessee
Pearl Merritt
Specialist
State Department of Education
Equal Vocational Opportunity
213 Cordell Hull Building
Nashville, TN 37219
615-773-3423 (ph)
615-741-6236 (fax)

Texas
Christine Smart
Coordinator for Equal Access to Voc.
Ed.
Texas Education Agency
1701 N. Congress

Austin, TX 78701
512-463-9311 (ph)
512-475-3575 (fax)

Utah
Nadine Bunnell
Equal Opportunity Specialist
Utah State Office of Education
Division of Vocational Education
250 E. Fifth Street South
Salt Lake City, UT 84111
801-538-7858 (ph)
801-538-7868 (fax)

Vermont
Mary Mulloy
Consultant, Vocational Sex Equity
State Department of Education
PO Box 60
Montpelier, VT 05602
802-828-3101 (ph)
802-828-3140 (fax)

Virginia
Elizabeth Hawa
Associate in Vocational Gender
Equity
State Department of Education
PO Box 6Q
Richmond, VA 23216
804-225-2890 (ph)
804-371-8796 (fax)

Washington
Harriet VanDeursen
Vocational Sex Equity Coordinator
Office of Public Instruction
Old Capitol Bldg FL-11
State of Washington
Olympia, WA 98504
206-753-5651 (ph)
206-753-4515 (fax)

West Virginia
Sallie Helton
Vocational Education Sex Equity
Coordinator
State Department of Education
Capitol Complex, Room B-230
Charleston, WV 25305
304-348-3430 (ph)
304-348-0048 (fax)

Wisconsin
Frances Johnson
Sex Equity Coordinator
Wisconsin Board of Vocational,
Technical, and Adult Education
310 Price Place
Madison, WI 53707
608-266-1840 (ph)
608-266-1690 (fax)

Barbara L. Schuler
Vocational Equity Consultant
Wisconsin Dept. of Public Instruction
PO Box 7841
Madison, WI 53707-7841
608-267-9170 (ph)
608-267-1052 (fax)

Wyoming
Lois Mottonen
Gender Equity Coordinator
State Department of Education
Hathaway Building, Room 258
Cheyenne, WY 82002-0050
307-777-6276 (ph)
307-777-6234 (fax)

Appendix E
Equal Opportunity Commission Offices

Alabama
Equal Employment Opportunity
Commission
Birmingham District Office
1900 Third Avenue, North, Suite 101
Birmingham, Alabama 35203
205-731-0082

Arizona
Equal Employment Opportunity
Commission
Phoenix District Office
4520 North Central Avenue
Suite 300
Phoenix, Arizona 85012-1848
602-640-5000

Arkansas
Equal Employment Opportunity
Commission
Little Rock Area Office
320 West Capitol Avenue, Suite 621
Little Rock, Arkansas 72201
501-324-5060

California
Equal Employment Opportunity
Commission
Fresno Local Office
1313 P Street, Suite 103
Fresno, California 93721
209-487-5793

Equal Employment Opportunity
Commission
880 Front Street
Room 45-21
San Diego, California 92188
619-557-6288

Equal Employment Opportunity
Commission

Los Angeles District Office
3660 Wilshire Boulevard, Fifth Floor
Los Angeles, California 90010
213-251-7278

Equal Employment Opportunity
Commission
Oakland Local Office
1333 Broadway, Room 430
Oakland, California 94612
415-273-7588

Equal Employment Opportunity
Commission
San Francisco District Office
901 Market Street, Suite 500
San Francisco, California 94103
415-744-6500

Equal Employment Opportunity
Commission
San Jose Local Office
96 North Third Street, Suite 200
San Jose, California 95112
408-291-7352

Colorado
Equal Employment Opportunity
Commission
Denver District Office
1845 Sherman Street, Second Floor
Denver, Colorado 80203
303-866-1300

Washington, D.C.
Equal Employment Opportunity
Commission
Washington Field Office
1400 L Street NW, Suite 200
Washington, D.C. 20005
202-275-7377

Florida
Equal Employment Opportunity
Commission
Miami District Office
1 Northeast First Street, Sixth Floor
Miami, Florida 33132
305-536-4491

Equal Employment Opportunity
Commission
Tampa Area Office
Timberlake Federal Building Annex
501 East Polk Street, Suite 1020
Tampa, Florida 33602
813-228-2310

Georgia
Equal Employment Opportunity
Commission
Atlanta District Office
75 Piedmont Avenue, NE, Suite 1100
Atlanta, Georgia 30335
404-331-6093

Hawaii
Equal Employment Opportunity
Commission
Honolulu Local Office
677 Ala Moana Blvd., Suite 404
Honolulu, Hawaii 96813
808-541-3120

Illinois
Equal Employment Opportunity
Commission
Chicago District Office
536 South Clark Street, Room 930
Chicago, Illinois 60605
312-353-2713

Indiana
Equal Employment Opportunity
Commission
Indianapolis District Office
46 East Ohio Street

Room 456
Indianapolis, Indiana 46204
317-226-7212

Kentucky
Equal Employment Opportunity
Commission
Louisville Area Office
600 Martin Luther King Jr. Place,
Room 268
Louisville, Kentucky 40202
502-582-6082

Louisiana
Equal Employment Opportunity
Commission
New Orleans District Office
701 Loyola Avenue, Suite 600
New Orleans, Louisiana 70113
504-589-2329

Maryland
Equal Employment Opportunity
Commission
Baltimore District Office
111 Market Place, Suite 4000
Baltimore, Maryland 21202
301-962-3932

Massachusetts
Equal Employment Opportunity
Commission
Boston Area Office
1 Congress Street, Room 1001
Boston, Massachusetts 02114
617-565-3200

Michigan
Equal Employment Opportunity
Commission
Detroit District Office
477 Michigan Avenue, Room 1540
Detroit, Michigan 48226
313-226-7636

Minnesota
Equal Employment Opportunity
Commission
Minneapolis Local Office
220 Second Street South, Room 108
Minneapolis, Minnesota 55401-2141
612-370-3330

Mississippi
Equal Employment Opportunity
Commission
Jackson Area Office
Cross Road Building Complex
207 West Amite Street
Jackson, Mississippi 39201
601-965-4537

Missouri
Equal Employment Opportunity
Commission
Kansas City Area Office
911 Walnut Street, Tenth Floor
Kansas City, Missouri 64106
816-426-5773

Equal Employment Opportunity
Commission
St. Louis District Office
625 N. Euclid Street, Fifth Floor
St. Louis, Missouri 63108
314-425-6585

New Jersey
Equal Employment Opportunity
Commission
Newark Area Office
60 Park Place, Room 301
Newark, New Jersey 07102
201-645-63383

New Mexico
Equal Employment Opportunity
Commission
Albuquerque Area Office
505 Marquette, NW, Suite 1105

Albuquerque, New Mexico 87102-2189
505-766-2061

New York
Equal Employment Opportunity
Commission
Buffalo Local Office
28 Church Street, Room 301
Buffalo, New York 14202
716-846-4441

Equal Employment Opportunity
Commission
New York District Office
90 Church Street, Room 1501
New York, New York 10007
212-264-7161

North Carolina
Equal Employment Opportunity
Commission
Charlotte District Office
5500 Central Avenue
Charlotte, North Carolina 28212
704-567-7100

Equal Employment Opportunity
Commission
Greensboro Local Office
324 West Market Street, Room 27
PO Box 3363
Greensboro, North Carolina 27401
919-333-5174

Equal Employment Opportunity
Commission
1309 Annapolis Drive
Raleigh, North Carolina 27608
919-856-44064

Ohio
Equal Employment Opportunity
Commission
Cincinnati Area Office

The Ameritrust Building
525 Vine Street, Suite 810
Cincinnati, Ohio 45202
513-684-2851

Equal Employment Opportunity
Commission
Cleveland District Office
1375 Euclid Avenue, Room 600
Cleveland, Ohio 44115
216-522-2001

Oklahoma
Equal Employment Opportunity
Commission
Oklahoma City Area Office
531 Couch Drive
Oklahoma City, Oklahoma 73102
405-231-4911

Pennsylvania
Equal Employment Opportunity
Commission
Philadelphia District Office
1421 Cherry Street, Tenth Floor
Philadelphia, Pennsylvania 19102
215-656-7020

Equal Employment Opportunity
Commission
Pittsburgh Area Office
1000 Liberty Avenue, Room 2038-A
Pittsburgh, Pennsylvania 15222
412-644-3444

South Carolina
Equal Employment Opportunity
Commission
Greenville Local Office
15 South Main Street, Suite 530
Greenville, South Carolina 29601
803-241-4400

Tennessee
Equal Employment Opportunity
Commission
Memphis District Office
1407 Union Avenue, Suite 621
Memphis, Tennessee 38104
901-722-2617

Equal Employment Opportunity
Commission
Nashville Area Office
50 Vantage Way, Suite 202
Nashville, Tennessee 37228
615-736-5820

Texas
Equal Employment Opportunity
Commission
Dallas District Office
8303 Elmbrook Drive
Dallas, Texas 75247
214-767-7015

Equal Employment Opportunity
Commission
El Paso Area Office
The Commons Building C
Suite 103
4171 N. Mesa Street
El Paso, Texas 79902
915-534-6550

Equal Employment Opportunity
Commission
Houston District Office
1919 Smith Street, Seventh Floor
Houston, Texas 77002
713-653-3320

Equal Employment Opportunity
Commission
San Antonio District Office
5410 Frdericksburg Road, Suite 200
San Antonio, Texas 78229

Virginia
Equal Employment Opportunity
Commission
Norfolk Area Office
252 Monticello Avenue, First Floor
Norfolk, Virginia 23510
804-441-3470

Equal Employment Opportunity
Commission
Richmond Area Office
3600 West Broad Street, Room 229
Richmond, Virginia 23230
804-771-2692

Wisconsin
Equal Employment Opportunity
Commission
Milwaukee District Office
310 West Wisconsin Avenue
Suite 800
Milwaukee, Wisconsin 53203
414-297-1111

U.S. Department of Education
OCR
Mary E. Switzer Bldg.
330 C. Street, SW
Washington, D.C. 20202
202-205-5413

Appendix F
Other Gender Equity Resources

American Association of University
Women
2401 Virginia Avenue, NW
Washington, D.C. 20037
202-785-7700

American Bar Association
Commission on Women in the
Profession
750 North Lake Shore Drive
Chicago, IL 60611
312-988-5668

American Civil Liberties Union
Women's Rights Project
132 West 43rd Street
New York, NY 10036
212-944-9800

Asian-American Legal Defense and
Education Fund
99 Hudson Street
New York, NY 10013
212-966-5932

Asian Immigrant Women Advocates
310 8th Street, Suite 301
Oakland, CA 94607
510-268-0192

Assault
Box 21378
Washington, DC 20009
202-483-7165

Association of American Colleges
1818 R Street, NW
Washington, D.C. 20009
202-387-1300

Business and Professional
Women/USA

2012 Massachusetts Avenue, NW
Washington, D.C. 20036
202-293-1100

Center for Women and Policy Studies
2000 P Street, NW, Suite 508
Washington, DC 20036
202-872-1770

Coalition of Labor Union Women
15 Union Square
New York, NY 10003
212-242-0700

Equal Rights Advocates
1663 Mission Street, Suite 500
San Francisco, CA 94103
415-621-0505

Federally Employed Women Legal
and Education Fund
1400 Eye Street, NW
Washington, D.C. 20005
202-462-5253

Fund for the Feminist Majority
1600 Wilson Boulevard, Suite 704
Arlington, VA 22209
703-522-2501

"Kindness"
9307 West 74 Street
Merriam, KS 66204
913-432-5158

Lawyer's Committee for Civil Rights
Under the Law
1400 Eye Street, NW, Suite 400
Washington, D.C. 20005
202-321-1212

Mexican American Legal Defense and
Education Fund
1430 K Street, NW
Washington D.C. 20005
202-628-4074

Ms. Foundation for Women
Ad Hoc Sexual Harassment Coalition
141 Fifth Avenue
New York, NY 10010
212-353-8580

NAACP Legal Defense and
Educational Fund, Inc.
99 Hudson Street
New York, NY 10013
212-219-1900

National Association of
Commissions for Women
c/o D.C. Commission for Women
N-354 Reeves Center
2000 14th Street, NW
Washington, D.C. 20009
202-628-5030

National Association for Public
Interest Law
215 Pennsylvania Avenue
Washington, D.C. 20003
202-546-9707

National Association for Women in
Education
1325 18th Street, NW, Suite 210
Washington, D.C. 20036
202-659-9330

National Association of Working
Women: 9 to 5
1224 Hudson Road
Cleveland, OH 44113
216-566-9308

National Center for the Prevention
and Control of Rape
National Institutes for Mental Health
5600 Fishers Lane
Rockville, MD 20852
301-443-3728

National Conference of State
Legislatures Women's Network
1607 250th Avenue
Corwith, IA 50430
515-583-2156

National Council for Research on
Women
The Sara Delano Roosevelt Memorial
House
47-49 East 65 Street
New York, NY 10021
212-570-5001

National Employment Law Project
236 Massachusetts Avenue, NE
Washington, DC 20002
202-544-2185

NOW Legal Defense Fund
National Association of Women and
the Law
99 Hudson Street, 12th Floor
New York, NY 10013
212-925-6635

National Women's Law Center
1616 P. Street NW
Washington, DC 20036
202-328-5160

Office of Personnel Management
1900 E Street, NW
Washington, D.C. 20415
202-606-1212

Pacific Resource Development Group
4044 NE 58 the Street
Seattle, WA 98105

Quality Work Environments
P.O. Box 1946
Manhattan, KS 66502
913-532-5533

STOP Violence Coalition
9307 West 74 Street
Merriam, KS 66204
913-432-5158

Survival Skills Education and
Development
1640 Fairchild, Suite 4
Manhattan, KS 66502
(913)776-4902
FAX (913)537-017

Trial Lawyers for Public Justice
2000 P Street, NW, Suite 611
Washington, DC 20036
202-463-8600

United States Student Association
815 15th Street, NW, Suite 838
Washington, DC 20005
202-347-8772

Wider Opportunities for Women
1324 G Street, NW
Washington, DC 20005
202-638-3143

Women Employed Institutes
22 West Monroe, Suite 1400
Chicago, IL 60603
312-782-3902

Women Organized Against Sexual
Harassment
PO Box 4768
Berkeley, CA 94704

415-642-7310

Women Students' Sexual Harassment
Caucus
Department of Applied Psychology
Ontario Institute for Studies in
Education
252 Bloor Street West
Toronto, Ontario M5S 1V6

Women's Action for Good
Employment Standards
c/o Institute for Research on
Women's Health
1616 18th Street, NW, #109 B
Washington, DC 20009
202-483-8643

Women's Law Project
125 South 9th Street, Suite 401
Philadelphia, PA 19107
215-928-9801

Women's Legal Defense Fund
1875 Connecticut Avenue, NW
Suite 710
Washington, DC 20009
202-986-2600

Appendix G
Kids' Bill of Rights:

1. Kids have the right to be who they are.
2. Kids have the right to loved.
3. Kids have the right to be cared for when they're sick and well.
4. Kids have the right to be safe and protected.
5. Kids have the right to defend themselves when someone hurts them, and to get a grown-up to help.
6. Kids have the right to want and get attention and affection.
7. Kids have the right to be respected.
8. Kids have the right to make mistakes.
9. Kids have the right to get guidance from others.
10. Kids have the right to learn from others.
11. Kids have the right to ask questions.
12. Kids have the right to have feelings.
13. Kids have the right to say yes and no.
14. Kids have the right to choose what they like and don't like.
15. Kids have the right to agree and disagree with other kids and grown-ups.
16. Kids have the right to be with others sometimes.
17. Kids have the right to be alone sometimes.
18. Kids have the right to be different and unique.
19. No one has the right to physically hurt you--not grown-ups, not other kids.
20. No one has the right to sexually hurt you--not grown-ups, not other kids.

Reproduced by permission from Project Charlie, 4570 West 77th Street, Suite 198, Edina, MN 55435, 612-830-1432

Glossary of Terms

Although there are various definitions of each of the following terms, for the purpose of our discussion we will use the following:

Alienation
A state of estrangement from oneself, or society. Feminists argue that women's oppression in the home, in culture and in sexuality, creates a gender-specific form of women's alienation. And to the extent that men and women conform to stereotypes of masculinity and femininity, they will be alienated from each other in incompatible ways.

Androgyny
The psychological and psychic mixture of traditional masculine and feminine virtues comes from the Greek words andro (male) and gyn (female.) Many people believe that androgynous personalities are holistic and have a capacity to experience the full range of human emotions.

Constructive Notice
The employer under the conditions which existed should have known that sexual harassment was taking place; an implied notice.

Curriculum Theory
Although curriculum is usually thought of as a group of subjects based on disciplines operating a syllabus of material and a particular method of teaching. The overt and "hidden" curriculum are the conscious and unconscious ideology of any institution. Often the curriculum reinforces sex-role stereotyping by operating on a principle of "male as norm."

Equality
No individual should be less equal than any other. Judgements should be based upon individual merit rather than racial, ethnic, religious, social status, or gender.

Feminism
Feminism is an ideology of social transformation aimed at creating a world where women are liberated from all injustice because of their sex.

Hidden Curriculum

Education often includes material and messages that are not consciously planned. Often these messages reinforce sexual stereotyping. The hidden curriculum can include sex segregation in activities and programs or attitudes toward women exhibited by teachers and administrators.

Hostile Work Environment

Unwelcome sexual conduct that unreasonably interferes with an individual's school performance or creates an intimidating, hostile or offensive environment.

Gender

We distinguish between sex and gender. Sex is biological and gender is behavioral. You are born to a sex, however, many of the traits often associated with being male or female are actually created by social pressures and conditioning.

Non-Verbal Harassment

Displaying of material that is sexually suggestive such as pornographic photos, jokes, or drawings. It can also be following a person, leering at a person's body, writing unwanted letters, or giving unwanted gifts.

Physical Harassment

Touching yourself or another person in a suggestive sexual manner.

Priming

Specific stimuli in the school environment prime certain categories for the application of stereotypical thinking (i.e. availability of photographs of nude and partially nude women, sexual joking, and sexual slurs, etc.).

Quid Pro Quo

Submission to or rejection of sexual conduct by an individual is used as the basis for educational decisions affecting the individual (something for something).

Respondeat Superior Liability

The employer is held liable where the person responsible for the sexual harassment is a supervisor.

Sex Bias

Sex bias is the character of behavior and attitudes resulting from belief in sex stereotypes and/or adherence to restrictively defined sex roles. The stereotype that women are not active, not independent, not competent, not able to take care of themselves, and are in need of help and protection is widespread and finds expression in our school classrooms.

Sexism

Any social relationship where a person or group is denigrated because of their sex. Sexism limits the activities and opportunities of its victims. Sexual stereotyping is an example of sexism.

Sex-Role Identity

Among the major determinants of sex-role identification of a young child are perceptions of similarity to others, and the adoption of behaviors traditionally encouraged for his or her sex. Sex-role identity is the degree to which an individual self-identifies with what is generally believed or accepted to be appropriate as masculine or feminine roles.

Sexual or Sex-based Behavior

Some kind of sexual connotation to the behavior or the behavior occurs because of the person's sex.

Sexual Favoritism

A student receives opportunities or benefits as a result of submission to a teacher's sexual advances.

Sexual Harassment

Unwelcome sexual advances, requests for sexual favors, and other verbal or physical conduct of a sexual nature.

Sex-Role

In our society, a role is the behavior expected of the occupant of a given position or status. Sex-role is then the behavior expected of men or women on the basis of biological sex.

Sex-Role Stereotype

Sex-role stereotypes are standardized, oversimplified conceptions of the behaviors that are appropriate to females and males. Sex-role stereotyping consists of forming expectations for the behavior of individual females and males on the basis of these stereotypes. In the stereotyping of sex roles, the qualities of the individual are ignored. It is difficult to contradict the social expectations that lead to this devaluing of the individual, often because of the belief that stereotyped traits are inborn, natural.

Sex Typing
Sex-typed characteristics are those characteristics associated with males and females. The three classes of sex-typed characteristics are (1) physical attributes (i.e. boys should be strong and large and that girls are petite and pretty), (2) overt behavior (i.e. boys are loud, aggressive and outgoing and girls are quiet, passive and shy), and (3) feelings, attitudes, motives, and beliefs (i.e. boys don't cry or have the ability to nurture and girls are naturally nurturing and emotional.)

Stereotyping
Stereotyping refers to a tendency for a belief to be widespread in any social group or society (e.g., "Women are emotional, Men are analytical"). According to Mitchell, it also denotes an oversimplification of a belief in regard to its content together with a tendency for the belief to be resistant to factual evidence to the contrary. People believe that their concepts of any particular group (e.g., women, men, blacks, oriental, whites, etc.) are accurate representations of real individuals in the group, whereas their conception is actually a stereotype acquired in some way other than direct experience. Because people mainly see what they expect to see, the situation is usually not improved even by direct experience. Stereotyped concepts are usually:
1. Simple rather than complex or differentiated.
2. Erroneous rather than accurate.
3. Acquired second hand rather than through direct experience with the reality it is supposed to represent.
4. Resistant to modification by new experience.

Unwelcome Sexual Advances
Even though the employee or student submits to sexual advances, the criteria to determine whether sexual harassment occurred is whether the sexual advancement was unwelcome.

Verbal Harassment
Telling sexual jokes or stories, making sexual comments about a person's body, sexual propositions, sexually suggestive, or obscene comments.

References

Allport, G., (1954). *The Nature of Prejudice*, Garden City New York: Doubleday Anchor Books.

Andelin, H., (1992). *Facinating Womanhood*, New York: Bantam Books.

Beauvais, K. (1986). *Workshops to Combat Sexual Harassment: a Case Study of Changing Atituedes.* Signs: A Journal of Women in Culture and Society, *121*.

Benson, A., (1984). *Comment of Crocker's "An Analysis of Univesity Definitions of Sexual Harsassment."* Signs: Journal of Women in culture and Society, *9*.

Bernard, C., and Schlaffer, E, (1983). *The Man in the Street: Why He Harasses, in Feminist Frontiers, (eds.)* Richardson, L, and Taylor, V, Reading, Massachusetts: Addison-Wesley.

Bryant, A.,(1993). *The Year of the Woman Gives Hope to Our Nation's Schoolgirls Gender Equity in Education Act Unveiled,* news release, Washington, D.C.: American Association of University Women (April 21).

Cadoff, J., (1993). *How To Raise A Strong Daughter In A Man's World,* Twins, January/February.

Charren, P., (no date). Quoted in Cadoff, J., (1993). *How To Raise A Strong Daughter In A Man's World,Twins,*January.

Chodorow, N., (1971). *Being and Doing: A Cross Cultural Examination of Socialization of Males and Females,* in Gornick, V. and Moran, B. (eds.), Woman in Sexist Society, New York: Basic Books.

Chodorow, N., (1974). *Family Structure and Feminine Personality,* in Rosalado, M., and Lamphere, L. (eds.), Woman, Culture and Society. Stanford: Stanford University Press.

Coder-Mikinski, T., (1993). *Counselor Self-Efficacy and Suicide Intervention,* Unpublished Dissertation, University of Kansas.

Coopersmith, S., (1967). *Human Nature and the Social Order.* New York: Scribner.

David, D., and Brannon, R, (1976). *The Forty-nine Percent Majority: the Male Sex Role* , New York: Random House.

EEOC Guidance Memorandum 6 to Field Personnel, 57, L.W. 2261 (Oct. 17, 1988)

Eskenazi, M. and Gallen, D., (1992). *Sexual Harassment: Know Your Rights!*, New York, Carroll & Graf Publishers, Inc.

Farley, L., (1978). *Sexual Shakedown*, New York, NY: Warner Books.

Fine, J., (1987, August 24-30). *No Laughing Matter: Sexual Harassment is Serious Problem for Companies. Dallas Times Herald*, pp; 9-11.

First, P., (1992). *Educational Policy for School Administrators*, Boston: Allyn & Bacon.

Fiske, S., (1991). Testimony appearing as an expert witness on plaintiff's behalf in the case *Robinson v. Jacksonville Shipyards, Inc.* 760 F.Supp. 1486 (M.D.Fla. 1991) at 1502.

French, M., (1992). *The War Against Women*, New York: Ballantine Books.

Fried, S., (1993). Conversations with authors April and May.

Gilligan, C., (1982). *In a Different Voice: Psychological Theory and Women's Development.*, Cambridge, MA: Harvard Univerity Press.

Gleick, E., (1992). *The Boys On The Bus, People* Nov. 30, at 125.

Goldstein, L., (1992). *Feminist Jurisprudence*, Lanham, Maryland: Rowman & Littlefield Publishers, Inc.

Grauerholz, E., (1989). *Sexual Harassment of Women Professors by Students: Exploring the Dynamics of Power, Authority, and Gender in a University Setting.* Sex Roles, 21.

Hail, R., and Sandler, B., (no date). *The Classsroom Climate: A Chilly One For Women?* Paper published by the Project of the Status and Education of Women, Washington D.C.: Association of American Colleges.

Hamachek, D., (1978). *Encounters With The Self* (2nd ed.) New York: Holt, Rinehart and Winston.

Harding, J., (1968). *Stereotypes.* In O. Sills (Ed.) *International encyclopedia of the social sciences*, 15. New York: Crowell, Collier and MacMilian, Inc.

Hess, R., (1992). *Sexual Assault Cover-up in Public Schools.* FACT: Friends of Alachua County Talk, (May).

Hostile Hallways: The AAUW Survey on Sexual Harassment in America's Schools, (1993). Washington, D.C.: American Association of University Women Educational Foundation.

Hostile Hallways: The AAUW Survey on Sexual Harassment in America's Schools, (1993). (Fact Sheet) Washington, D.C.: American Association of University Women Educational Foundation.

Hubbard-Harris, V., (1993). Conversation with the authors.

Johnson, C, Stockdale, M, Saal, F, (1991). *Persistence of Men's Misperceptions of Friendly Cues Across a Variety of Interpersonal Encounters,* Psychology of Women Quarterly, 15 (1991) at 464.

Johnson, K. and Workman, J, (1992), *Clothing and Attributions Concerning Sexual Harasment*, Home Economics Research Journal, Vol. 21, No. 2, December, p. 161.

Jordan, J., (1986). *The Meaning of Mutuality*, Work In Progress # 23, Wellesley, MA: The Stone Center, Wellesley College.

Kagan, J., (1964). *Acquisition of Sex Typing and Sex-Role Idenity*. In Hoffmen, M & Hoffmen, L., (Ed.) *Review of Child Development Research*. New York: Russsell Sage Foundation.

Kaplan, H., (1975). *Self-Attitudes and Deviant Behavior*, Pacific Palisades, CA: Goodyear Publishing.

Kenig, J., and Ryan, *Sex Differences in Levels of Tolerance and Attribution of Blame for Sexual Harassment on a University Campus*, Sex Roles, 15, at 535.

LeClair, L., (1991). *Sexual Harassment Between Peers Under Title VII and TItle IX Why Girls Just Can't Wait to be Working Women*, Vermont Law Review, Vol. 6:30.

Lever, J., (1978). *Sex differences in the Complexity of Children's Games*, American Sociological Review.

Lever, J., (1976). *Sex Differences in the Games Children Play*, Social Problems.

Lewis, J., Hastings, S., and Morgan, A.,(1993). *Sexual Harassment in Education, National Organizaiton on Legal Problems of Education*, Topeka, Kansas.

Mackinnon, C., (1979). *Sexual Harassment of Working Women: A Case of Sex Discriminination*, New Haven: Yale University Press.

Manning, A., *School Girls Sexually Harassed*, USA Today, Wednesday, March 24, 1993, p1A.

Masters, A., (1992). *The Evolution of the Legal Concept of Environmental Sexual Harassment of U.S. Higher Education Students By Faculty*, Unpublished Dissertation, University of Florida.

McClelland, D., (1974). *Power: The Inner Experience*, New York: Irvington Press

Mead, M., (1968).*Sex and Temperament in Three Primitive Societies,* New York: Dell, first published in 1935.

Mead, M., (1978), *A Proposal: We Need Tabos On Sex at Work. Redbook* (April).

Mitchell, G. (1968). *A Dictionary of Sociology.* Chicago: Aldine Publishing Co.

Money, J. and Ehrhardt, A., (1972). *Man and Woman, Boy and Girl,* Baltimore:Johns Hopkins University Press

Omilian, S., (1987). *Sexual Harassment in Employment*, Deerfield, Illinois: Callaghan.

O'Gorman Hughes, J. and Sandler, B., (1988). *Peer Harassment: Hassles for Women on Campus*, Washington, D.C.: Project on the Status and Education of Women, Association of American Colleges.

O'Gorman Hughes, J. and Sandler, B., (1992) *In Case of Sexual Harassment: A guide for Women Students*, Washington, D.C.: Center for Women Policy Studies.

Palin, P., (1993). Mr. Palin is the Human Resources Manager for the South Washington County Schools, Cottage Grove, Minnesota. Conversations and written communication with the authors during the period between April 1, 1993 to April 28, 1993.

Pauldi, M. and Barickman, R., (1991). *Academic and Workplace Sexual Harassment*, Albany: State University of New York Press.

Petrocelli, W. and Repa, B., (1992). *Sexual Harassment On The Job*, Berkely, Claifornia: Nolo Press.

Piaget , J., (1965). *The Moral Judgement Of The Child*, New York: The Free Press.

Preventing Sexual Harassment in Utah State Government, (1989). Department of Human Resource Management, State of Utah.

Rauch, C., Sandquist, L., Stokes, A., (1993). Conversations and communications with the authors regarding the program on eradicating sexual harassment that has been implemented at Goodrich Middle School, Lincoln, NE.

Rosenberg, M. (1965). *Conceiving The Self,* New York: Basic Books.

Rubin, L., (1992). *Sexual Harassment: Individual Differences In Reporting Behaviors,* Unpublished doctoral dissertation, University of Kansas.

Saal, F., Johnson, C., & Weber, N. *"Friendly or Sexy?" It May Depend On Whom You Ask." Psychology of Women Quarterly,* 13, at 263-276.

Salomone, R., (1986).*Equal Education Under Law,* New York, St. Martin's Press.

Sandroff, R., (1992). *Sexual Harassment: The Inside Story, Working Woman Magazine,* (June).

Schneider (1987). *Graduate Women, Sexual Harassment and University Policy*, Journal of Higher Education, Vol 58. 46-65.

School Safety & the Legal Commuity, (1985). Westlake Village, CA: National School Safety Center.

Sexual Harassment in the Federal Government: An Update, A Report of the U.S. Merit Systems Protection Board Office of Merit Systems Review and Studies, Washington, D.C., June, 1988.

Sexual Harassment in the Federal Workplace, A Report of the U.S. Merit Systems Protection Board Office of Merit Systems Review and Studies, Washington, D.C., March 1981.

Shoop, R., and Edwards, D, (1992). *"Training Manual"* tthat accompanies the video program Sexual Harassment: *What is It and Why Should I Care?*, Manhattan, KS: Quality Work Environments, Inc.

Shoop, R., and Hellebust, L., (1983). *How To Get What You Want From Your State Legislature*, Manhattan, KS: Kansas Center for Community Education.

Shrauger, J. & Lund, A. (1975). *Self-Evaluation And Reactions To Evaluations From Others. Journal of Personality*, 43.

Silva, T., (1992). *Students Tell Board of Sexual Harassment,* Gainesville Sun, (May 6).

Stein, N., Marshall, N., and Trop, L., (1993). *Secrets In Public: Sexual Harassment In Our Schools.* A report on the results of a *Seventeen* magazine survey. Center for Research on Women, Wellesley College.

Stoller, R., (1964). A Contribution To The Study Of Gender Idenity, *International Journal of Psycho-Analysis 45*, 220-226.

Surry, J. and Bergman, S., (1992). *The Woman-Man Relationship: Impasses and Possibilities*, Work In Progress # 55, Wellesley, MA: The Stone Center, Wellesley College.

Tannen, D., (1990). *You Just Don't Understand,* New York: Ballantine Books.

The AAUW Report: *How Schools Shortchange Girls,* (1992). Washington, D.C.: American Association of University Women Educational Foundation

Thurston, L., (1993). Conversations with authors.

Till, F. J. (1980). *Sexual Harassment: A Report On The Sexual Harassmesnt Of Students.* Report of the National Advisory Council on Women's Educational Programs. Washington D.C: U.S. Department of Education.

Unell, B., (1993). Conversations with authors during April and May.

Walsh, C., (1993). *Openly Addressing Sexual Harassment In Schools,* School Safety Update, Westlake Village, CA: National School Safety Center, (April).

Webb, S., (1992). *Preventing Sexual Hrassment In A Small Business,* Small Business Forum, (Fall).

Webb, S., (1991). *Sexual Harassment: Investigator's Manual* Premiere Publishing, Ltd.

Webb, S., (1991). *Step Forward: Sexual Harassment In The Workplace*, Mastermedia.

Williams, R., and Williams, V., (1993). *Anger Kills,* New York: Times Books.

About the Authors

Robert J. Shoop is a professor of Educational Law at Kansas State University. He is the author of six books, over 100 journal articles, and several monographs and book chapters on various legal issues. His most recent books are, *School Law for the Principal: A Handbook for Practitioners,* and *A Primer for School Risk Management* , both published by Allyn and Bacon.

He is the Co-founder and President of Quality Work Environments, Incorporated, a production and consulting company that has recently produced *Sexual Harassment: What Is It and Why Should I Care?* a video program on eliminating sexual harassment in the public schools. He is much sought as a speaker at national conferences and is a recognized authority in the area of legal issues in education and sexual harassment.

Dr. Shoop is a recipient of the Kansas State University Outstanding Teacher Award and is a member of the Board of Directors of the National Organization on Legal Problems of Education.

Jack W. Hayhow, Jr. is founder and President of Video Training, Incorporated. The company's primary business is development, production, and marketing of video based training programs.

Hayhow is author/narrator of the nationally acclaimed audio tape program and seminar entitled *Quit Wasting Your Money on Advertising.* He is the creator of the audio newsletter *In-Business* and the video based training program, *Selling Retail.* He is the executive producer of *Varsity Management* by Gallup, Incorporated and co-author/producer of *Sexual Harassment: What Is It and Why Should I Care?* by Quality Work Environments, Inc. *Success* magazine calls Hayhow's work "a head start on the competition!"

Prior to founding Video Training, he founded and was the president of Broadcast Marketing Group. Under his direction, BMG became the industry leader in audience building and sales promotion programs for radio stations. Clients included noted broadcast companies such as Lin Broadcasting, Viacom, Sconnix and Shamrock (Disney.) Hayhow began his career in the advertising agency business serving clients such as McDonald's Restaurants, Westin Hotels, Lee Jeans and Wendy's Old Fashioned Hamburgers.

Also Available

Sexual Harassment: What Is It and Why Should I Care a video program on eradicating sexual harassment from schools.

To order, to receive a catalogue, or to receive information abo consulting, write:

Quality Work Environments, Inc.

P.O. Box 1945
Manhattan, KS 66502
913-532-5533